Hungarian American Toledo

Life and Times in Toledo's Birmingham Neighborhood

Edited by
Thomas E. Barden
&
John Ahern

University of Toledo Urban Affairs Center

Manufactured in the United States of America

Barden, Thomas E. and Ahern, John

Hungarian American Toledo

Life and Times in Toledo's Birmingham Neighborhood

Includes bibliographical references and an index

ISBN 0-932259-02-2

Hungarian American Toledo is supported by funding from

the Hungarian Reformed Federation of America.

Contents

Preface

In his final public lectures, the late Chaim Potok began by reminding his audience that "each and every one of us is born into a small and particular world." *Hungarian American Toledo* is about one such world—the Hungarian ethnic neighborhood in Toledo, Ohio. Named for the great industrial center in the English midlands, Toledo's Birmingham neighborhood began to develop in the 1890s with the steel, copper, and shipbuilding industries that thrived on the east bank of the Maumee River.

Now, more than a hundred years later, Birmingham's heyday is over—the marching bands have disbanded and one no longer hears Hungarian spoken on every street corner. Toledo even decided a sign was needed to inform outsiders that they are entering the "Birmingham Ethnic Neighborhood."

Yet, unlike the other once-vibrant Toledo neighborhoods of German and Irish immigrants, Birmingham continues to maintain strong community cohesion. Even those who no longer live there remain loyal, returning regularly for festivals, weddings, church services, and often just to drive around the old streets and recapture it in their memories.

Our aim in *Hungarian American Toledo* has been to bring together the best research that has been done on this important ethnic American neighborhood. Our overall goal is to answer the seemingly simple question—what was it like to be born, grow up, and live in the Birmingham neighborhood?

The question was initially taken up in *Roots in Birmingham,* a locally published volume of oral histories collected by John Ahern in 1997. Realizing that a substantial body of research and writing existed about the neighborhood, we concluded that adapting these more scholarly materials would make a good fit with the grass-roots views presented by the oral histories of *Roots in Birmingham.* The publication of this volume makes the Birmingham community available to readers "inside and out."

There is no single methodology in *Hungarian American Toledo*; the reader won't find the word "deconstruction" on any of its pages or any monolithic theory of ethnicity espoused by the authors. Nor were the essays selected for their theoretical underpinnings. Rather, we have attempted to assemble a composite view of Birmingham, a collage rather than a diagram, time-line, or cultural model.

The introduction is written by the editors with input from Andrew Ludanyi, a historian at Ohio Northern University who has studied Birmingham for many years. It is also based on data from Yolanda Danyi Szuch's locally published *History of St. Stephen's Church*. We wanted to give an omniscient narrator's tour of the territory, a bird's eye overview. While social historians have long argued that such "history from the top down" is inadequate to understanding a time and place, we feel that it is a necessary beginning for a full grasp of the subsequent essays.

Hungarian American Toledo includes works by scholars and writers who have studied the Birmingham neighborhood from various perspectives: architectural, folkloristic, theatrical, historical, sociological, and photographic. Each essay features some aspect of the neighborhood in detail. We are especially pleased to include the late Raymond Pentzell's article on the Abauj Betlehemes jaték folk play because this thorough revision of his original article was his last work before his untimely death in 1996. We are also pleased to include an account of a 56er, one of the brave immigrants who made their way to Toledo after the failed Hungarian Revolt of 1956.

We hope this collage of perspectives and methods will bring the Birmingham experience to life for readers. The problem confronting such a project, of course, is that the past is not just words and pictures; it is a fleeting reality that passes once and can never be fully captured in a book. Yet words, ideas, and pictures are the only tools we have. We hope that those who know and love Birmingham will recognize it in these pages and that those who do not will be able at least to get a better glimpse of this "small and particular" American place.

* * * * *

Many people and organizations supported and encouraged the publication of *Hungarian American Toledo*. We want to thank the authors who contributed their outstanding work; the members of the University of Toledo Humanities Institute's Senior Fellows Seminar who helped us think our way to the volume's current form; Dr. Patrick McGuire, director of the UT Urban Affairs Center, who believed in our project from the beginning and put resources behind it; Molly Schiever Behrmann, whose creative design skills and editor's eye have made a handsome as well as readable book; The Toledo Lucas-County Public Library and its board for its strong support of the Birmingham Cultural Center, and William Puskas, Jr. and the Hungarian Reformed Federation of America, who provided grant support for research and publication preparation costs.

Tom Barden dedicates this book to his dear friend, the late Dr. Ray Pentzell, who would have loved to see it completed.

"A sausagey good evening to you, Ray."

John Ahern dedicates it to his wife, Lady Ann,

his son Mark who will be teaching about Birmingham,

his son Matt who lives on Valentine Street,

and all his friends from Birmingham—especially Judy, Imre,

Baba, Andy, Cathy, Pauline, Dee, Steve,

Barbara, Lillian, Millie,

departed friends John and Bette,

and also a special new friend of his family, Dr. Bill Horvath.

Introduction

From the beginning, Birmingham's strategic location near the mouth of the Maumee River made it naturally attractive to settlers in northwest Ohio. Even before the first Europeans arrived, Native American tribes were drawn to the area by its easy access to Lake Erie, its abundant fresh fish, and its location under a major migratory bird route. What would become the Birmingham neighborhood was settled early on by French, German, and Irish farmers impressed with the area's rich loamy soil. Streets and park names such as Collins, Valentine, and Paine commemorate these early farming settlers.

Birmingham's economic shift from agriculture to industry happened suddenly, beginning with the establishment of a foundry by the National Malleable Castings Company. In 1890, the company transferred approximately two hundred Hungarian workers from its home plant in Cleveland to its new East Toledo site on Front Street. Their arrival is documented in the Sacred Heart Catholic Church registers, where many of the first Hungarian settlers recorded their baptisms, marriages, and deaths until St. Stephen's Church was built in 1899. This dating is also confirmed in a 1941 profile of Hungarian-American communities in the United States by the Cleveland Hungarian daily newspaper *Szabadság (Freedom)*. Birmingham quickly became a working-class Hungarian enclave.

Local records show that most of the populace had emigrated from the so-called Palóc counties of North-Central Hungary: Heves, Abauj, and Gömör (now in Slovakia). Most, though far from all, were Roman Catholic. Although assigned to nearby Sacred Heart Church, the newly arrived Cleveland Hungarians were visited regularly by a Hungarian priest from Cleveland. In 1898, their own parish was established, the Church of St. Stephen, King of Hungary. Its registry listed about one hundred families in the following year.

Birmingham's name, like that of the Iron Town

neighborhood just to its north, was meant to invoke a thriving iron and steel manufacturing center. And by the time of World War I, it did resemble its English namesake, as National Malleable had been joined by United States Malleable, Maumee Malleable Castings, two coal yards, a cement-block manufactory, and the Rail Light Company (later Toledo Edison). The population of East Toledo was growing rapidly, too, going from 17,935 in the 1900 census to 39,836 in 1920. With this increase came civic amenities such as sidewalks, paved streets, grocery and dry good stores, banks, bakeries, and saloons. Often, the owners of these establishments lived above the store.

The ethnicity of East Toledo and Birmingham in particular continued as the total population increased. The number of Hungarian births in East Toledo grew from 647 in 1900 to 3,041 in 1920. The main ethnic group in Birmingham remained Hungarian, but others were present as well. Immigrant Slovaks, Czechs, Germans, Poles, Bulgarians, and Italians all appear in the World War I-era census records.

Like the Hungarians, other immigrants lived in modest homes built by real-estate speculators. What preservationists would later call "worker cottages" were small one-story houses without basements or indoor plumbing. The backyards were small and front lawns smaller. Some sites had smokehouses, and most residents kept chickens in fenced-in areas. In time, the privies were torn down and indoor sanitary facilities added.

At first, most homes had no front porches but that changed quickly and front-porch socializing became an important element of Birmingham life. Gardening occurred in a green-belt commons area along the railroad tracks marking the eastern and northern boundaries. Many Birmingham houses also became sources of revenue as families took in boarders, usually single male workers who paid rent to live with established families until they were able to start households of their own.

Until World War I, the major challenges facing the

first wave of immigrants were adjusting to their new work, neighborhood, and language. Here the role of the religious institutions was crucial. Some early organizational efforts came from religious societies, which would eventually become the basis for the neighborhood churches.

The first important society was the King Matthias Sick and Benevolent Society (Mátyás Király Egylet), which provided the equivalent of social security and disability insurance for members through dues and fund-raising. The association split when Catholic members established their own Saint Stephen (Szent István) Roman Catholic Society.

This move was followed by the formation of the Saint Michael's Greek Catholic Sick and Benefit Society and the John Calvin Society for Hungarian Reformed Protestants. In terms of community support and fund raising, the Society of Reformed Women and the Saint Elizabeth Roman and Greek Catholic Women's Society were equally important. These groups were the pre-World War I foundation on which the neighborhood's three churches—Roman

Catholic, Byzantine Catholic, and Hungarian Reform—were built.

Birmingham's own neighborhood school came early in its history. The first public-record mention is in 1894, in the annual report of the Toledo Public Schools: "Near the Craig Shipyard on the east side of the river in a settlement known as Birmingham, a four room brick building was erected which is now wholly occupied, furnishing ample school facilities for the people of this neighborhood."

Miss Lillian Patterson is listed as the school's principal in 1899, at a salary of $750 a year. By 1916, the Birmingham School was sixteen rooms in size. A gymnasium and classrooms were added in 1926. In 1962, the original building was torn down and replaced by the current structure on Paine Avenue. Throughout this period, the school was a social and educational center, used for public gatherings and adult night classes in reading and writing.

The pre-WWI era was also the heyday of Birmingham's military marching bands, the first of which was assembled in 1903. John Lengyel and later Julius Bertok were the organizers of these musical ensembles, which served social and ethnic purposes as well as patriotic and musical ones. The most impressive was the Rákóczy Band, named after Prince Francis Rákóczy II, who led the anti-Hapsburg rebellion of 1703-1712. The band, dressed in genuine Hungarian military uniforms, performed in Courthouse Park in Toledo and in Cleveland as part of the dedication of the Louis Kossuth Monument.

Social forces outside of Birmingham started to gain influence during this period. The Americanization Movement, a nativist response to the mass European immigration to Northern industrial cities, was exerting subtle—and sometimes not so subtle—pressure on ethnic communities around the country to conform to an "Anglo" model. Israel Zangwill's 1908 hit play, *The Melting Pot,* notwithstanding, the Americanization Movement urged immigrants to forsake their ethnic identity and abandon old-country loyalties. In Birmingham major pressure came from the secular

Birmingham School and a citizenship drive that took on a particularly aggressive tone during World War I.

These pressures can be seen in the speech Superintendent William B. Guitteau gave in 1916 to mark the opening of the enlarged sixteen-room brick building of the Birmingham School. After comparing the school opening to the launching of a great ship at the Toledo shipyard, Guitteau noted that several men had taken out naturalization papers and several more had enlisted in the Army or Navy, "thereby proving their loyalty to the country of their adoption."

He went on to say that "each year brings to us thousands and hundreds of thousands of Germans and Irishmen and Russians and Italians and Hungarians. And yet we have no German-Americans, no Irish-Americans, no Hungarian-Americans. We are all Americans, whether born here or abroad."

For the first generation of immigrants in Birmingham and around the country, this was the constant message—Americanize! Americanization meant Anglo-conformity. It wasn't until the rise of multi-cultural identity in the 1960s that this message was questioned and a more pluralistic idea of society emerged, one that saw America metaphorically more like a tossed salad than a melting pot.

* * * * *

The United States' entry into World War I provided an especially trying test of Birmingham's loyalties. As with German-Americans, this was also a difficult time for Hungarian-Americans. Their old homelands were now at war with their new country, forcing them to prove their American patriotism and loyalty. Acquiring citizenship and purchasing Liberty Bonds were two of the easiest ways to do this. A neighborhood businessman named János (John) Strick, for instance, was named the "first citizen of Toledo" for purchasing $20,000 worth of Liberty Bonds during the war.

Commitments to the new homeland were reinforced by the post-war dismemberment of the historic political units of East-Central Europe. The Austro-Hungarian empire vanished from the map, and citizens of northeastern Hungary found themselves living in the southeastern region of the newly created Czechoslovakia. Many in Birmingham no longer had a homeland to return to. Many residents were convinced that their future had been decided by the war. Like it or not, they were now destined to be Americans.

The period between the world wars was thus one of neighborhood consolidation and psychological adjustment to life in America. Changes in U.S. immigration laws that ended large-scale immigration combined with post-war realities to discourage any thought of returning to Hungary. A generation was coming into its own that had learned the assimilation lesson and had grown up speaking primarily English.

Birmingham's secular organizations and its three established churches encouraged neighborhood residents to secure American citizenship, become fluent in English, and get involved in American society and politics. Second-generation Birmingham residents broke into the American mainstream through the professions, business, and politics. The 1920s and 1930s saw the rise of such Hungarian-American-owned businesses as Kinsey's (Kigyossy's) Funeral Home, the Weizer furniture store, and Tony Packo's restaurant.

Birmingham did not escape the effects of the Great Depression, but the neighborhood's cohesion, the support of its churches and social organizations, and the overall spirit of kinship and solidarity helped most of the residents through the hard times. People took care of each other and the community institutions supported their efforts, including those where coal was "liberated" from trains coming through Birmingham with the tacit blessing of the priests.

Two prime movers in sustaining Hungarian consciousness during this period were Monsignor Elmér Eördögh and Dr. Géza Farkas. Elmér Géza Eördögh was born in Kassa, Hungary (now Kosice, Slovakia) on July 4,

1875, into a family tracing its roots to 1232 when King Andrew II of the House of Árpád ennobled them. Eördögh had a university education, including seminary training at Kalocsa, and was ordained a priest in 1897 at the age of 22.

Initially he worked in a Slovak and German parish in Hungary. He came to the United States in 1911 and, after a stay in Throop, Pennsylvania, he arrived in Toledo in 1913 and was installed as St. Stephen's pastor. From the beginning, Father Eördögh put his heart and soul into his assignment. Though plans for a large new church building had been made before his arrival, he took charge as the actual construction and fund-raising began. Until his death, Father Eördögh provided the church's goals and the strategies to achieve them. Almost all of the present structure was built under his supervision.

After World War I, Father Eördögh's family fell victim to Hungary's dismemberment when his brother and sister were separated by the new international borders. Since he himself associated home with upper Hungary, now part of Czechoslovakia, his commitment to staying in Toledo was reinforced. In spite of his strong links to an aristocratic past in Hungary, henceforth Father Eördögh would be a Hungarian-American priest.

His mission became more inextricably intertwined with the fate of the working people of Birmingham. He was still an Old-World, upper-class man in his personal habits, his ability to "wine and dine" guests, and in the selection of some of his official visitors, including such luminaries as Countess Bethlen, Otto von Hapsburg, and Joseph Cardinal Mindszenty.

Father Eördögh saw the parish as his primary concern, but even here his mode of operating was still old school. He was a hard taskmaster and a strict disciplinarian, establishing a nine p.m. curfew for the parish children. He managed to keep the youngsters, at least until they were sixteen, out of the local saloons. The force of his personality alone was enough to keep most of his congregation within the behavioral limits he personally defined.

Recognition came from the Toledo city fathers, prominent citizens of Birmingham, the Church hierarchy, and even officials in his former homeland. He became Monsignor Eördögh in 1929, and received Hungary's second highest award, the Hungarian Order of Merit, for his work on behalf of Hungarian-American immigrants. In 1938, he became chairman of the U.S. Hungarian contingent at the International Eucharistic Congress; in 1939, he was appointed the U.S. representative to the St. Ladislaus (László) Society of Hungary. Msgr. Eördögh offered his Golden Jubilee Mass on Nov. 16, 1947. But ill health began to take its toll, and during the last eight years of his life, assistant pastors took over most of his responsibilities.

The other seminal figure in this period was Dr. Géza Farkas, editor and publisher of the Hungarian-American newspaper *Toledo,* started in 1929. A first-generation immigrant who received his formal education in Hungary, Farkas shared the newspaper editing work with his wife, Rózsa, until her death in 1948. After that he worked alone, often setting his own type to bring *Toledo* to its readers.

Born in 1878 to upper middle-class parents in the western Hungarian town of Egerszeg in Zala County, Farkas initially considered the priesthood, but soon turned to legal studies and received a law degree in 1899 from Pázmány Péter University in Budapest. The law lost its appeal, however, and he began to work for newspapers.

Farkas visited the United States in 1904. He'd planned a brief stay, but settled in Cleveland and within a short time, became the city editor of its *Magyar Napilap (The Daily Hungarian)*. In 1908 he moved to Toledo where he worked for the Imperial Austro-Hungarian Consulate and started a steamship ticket and foreign exchange agency, becoming a major travel agent in Birmingham. He quickly entered national politics, too, serving as the Hungarian-American manager of William Howard Taft's 1908 presidential campaign. In 1911, Farkas became an American citizen.

Between 1908 and 1929, Farkas advised the Birmingham community on legal, personal, and even family matters. He was an active and public-spirited citizen who helped his people organize churches, fraternal societies, and benefits for the sick and poor. He was also a respected Birmingham spokesman and an important link between the Hungarian community and city authorities.

Farkas's many-sided but practical personality was mirrored in the pages of *Toledo*. It was not a sophisticated paper but a simple weekly concerned with providing working people with useful information. Beginning publication at the start of the Great Depression, *Toledo* remained the sole voice of the Hungarian-American community until the end of 1971. Forty years of history are reflected in its pages, including the perspectives of the editor and the reactions of his readers to World War II, the Soviet occupation and communization of Hungary, the Korean conflict, and the 1956 Hungarian Revolution. *Toledo* also covered events in the civic life of the city and state, interweaving them with the day-to-day concerns of Birmingham's churches, clubs, businesses, and cultural institutions.

Even though cultural assimilation continued, Hungarian customs, festivals, and food practices also thrived in Birmingham during these decades. It was not contradictory to be a fiercely patriotic American while maintaining traditions from the old country. The customs were not practiced in any conscious effort to preserve the Hungarian heritage. They were simply the way one lived life.

* * * * *

Birmingham greeted summer with the Corpus Christi procession. Young girls in white dresses and boys in their best clothes marched down the streets to pray at highly decorated outdoor altars set up in front of homes. Flowers were scattered on the streets and tree trunks were painted white to make the neighborhood look cleaner.

Autumn meant the Harvest Dance, to celebrate the crops taken from backyard and vacant-lot gardens. Children dressed in traditional costumes and marched behind a bandwagon (later a truck) to inform everyone that Harvest Dance was that night. At the dance hall, grapes were strung from a temporary arbor, and the adults danced the Csárdás. They attempted to steal the grapes as they danced, while the children were responsible for arresting the culprits. Everyone was caught and brought before the "judge," who levied a fine. The proceeds always went to a worthy neighborhood cause.

Christmas was not only the celebration of Christ's birth, and the occasion for bringing out the best Hungarian food, sweets, and delicacies, but also the time the Betlehemes folk play was enacted on the streets, in the bars and in neighborhood homes, and finally at midnight Mass on Christmas Eve. The players would collect donations of food, drink, and money from their audiences. [A complete text of the play begins on page 226.]

The feast of St. Patrick was also a major celebration in Birmingham. While many Toledoans flocked to the local bars to celebrate Ireland's patron saint, March 17 found the people of St. Stephen's participating in a solemn ceremony honoring the Virgin Mary and celebrating the Hungarians' Irish Madonna, whose feast coincidentally falls close to Hungarian Independence Day, March 15.

An interesting and little-known story lies behind this celebration. During the English Civil War, 1640-1660, the British persecution of Catholics in Ireland forced many Irish clergymen to escape to mainland Europe. A man named Bishop Lynch was given sanctuary by the Bishop of Györ in Hungary and was made an auxiliary bishop of that diocese. After Bishop Lynch's death, it was reported that a painting he had given his benefactors was seen to sweat blood for three hours. Toledo's bishop gave a copy of the painting to St. Stephen's Church, which led to the adoption of Ireland's patron saint in a Hungarian parish.

Easter was a tradition-rich time in Birmingham as well. On Palm Sunday, parishioners at St. Stephen's brought pussy willows to church to be blessed as they had done in Hungary where palms were unavailable. On the

Saturday before Easter, baskets of Easter food wrapped in native embroidery were brought to the church to be blessed. Easter eggs were decorated in the traditional folk manner. Easter was a time of jubilation, when the fasting and sacrifices of Lent were over.

The climax of the season was Easter Sunday Mass, but the folk customs continued into the next week. Easter Monday was dousing day, a tradition that originated in the villages of Hungary. Originally, the young men would throw buckets of water on the young women or pick them up and drop them in horse-watering troughs. In Birmingham, however, the ritual became more stylized and more dignified. Young men would ask to sprinkle the young lady of the house, sometimes with a bottle of perfume and sometimes with a homemade concoction. In some cases, they would enter the bedroom and sprinkle the girl before she awoke.

But the most common setting, especially among family members, was the breakfast table while outsiders, including potential or actual boyfriends, gathered at the front door. Often the sprinklers were given coins or Easter eggs. Dousing became an excuse for the younger boys to throw water balloons at the girls. Tuesday was the girls' turn to douse. It is said that even the U.S. Mail carriers stayed away from Birmingham on Easter Tuesday.

As was true in most European and American ethnic communities, social rites of passage, like the seasonal events, were centered around the church. Births were marked with baptisms; young adulthood was recognized by Confirmation and the biggest celebrations surrounded weddings. Divorce was extremely rare. Marriage was for keeps and for bearing children.

Once a marriage was announced, Birmingham residents watched for male members of the wedding party to walk the neighborhood with a ceremonial cane tied with ribbons proclaiming the event. Some wedding celebrations lasted for days. Gypsy orchestras played as beer and wine flowed freely. Father Eördögh, in fact, confined weddings to the early days of the week so St. Stephen's parishioners would not still be suffering from too much celebrating by the time of Sunday Mass.

The bells of St. Stephen were rung when a member of the congregation died, one sequence for a man and another for a woman. At the vigil, men stayed in the deceased's home guarding the body in tribute to their lost friend. During the night they would talk of their loss while playing cards, telling stories, and drinking. After the funeral service, especially if the person had been important or affluent, a band would lead the procession to the cemetery.

* * * * *

World War II brought profound changes to Birmingham. Some of these were part of the natural process during which the first American-born generation breaks away from the ways of their parents. Their children, reconciled to the past but fully Americanized, moved more smoothly into the mainstream society. The number of Birmingham residents becoming citizens in 1941 doubled from the previous year. The numbers remained high throughout World War II.

While the old Hungarian traditions did not die out, a marked community reaction against old-country, ethnic consciousness set in. Hungary was once again on the side of the enemy while the general American patriotism was surging. This attitude is apparent in a series of articles in *Toledo*, sponsored by the Common Council for American Unity and designed to give guidelines on raising children not hindered by local, parochial attitudes, but who would view issues globally. The articles warned against being "hamstrung by ethnic or neighborhood loyalties."

The socio-economic upheaval of the war years also changed Birmingham. Young women, housewives, and mothers left the home for the first time to staff the war industries while their boyfriends and husbands were drafted and shipped to far-off locales. These experiences re-oriented both groups, connecting them to different ethnic peer groups in the military and in the work place. The family and the local community were no longer their only social influences, and a wider view of the world inevitably resulted.

Broadened horizons and attitudinal changes were accelerated by the general technological transformation of American life in the post-war period. Like most Americans, Birmingham residents were moving up and out, with the automobile and television showing the way. People could drive out of the neighborhood in their cars and shop elsewhere, or even move to other parts of the city. This newfound mobility facilitated a migration to the suburbs, particularly to the nearby suburbs of Oregon and Rossford. The June 15, 1945, headline of *Toledo* proclaimed the departure of one of Birmingham's foremost citizens: "Strick János kiköltözik a magyar negyedünkből" . . . "John Strick is moving out of our Hungarian neighborhood."

Television's effect was more subtle. Its premiere in the neighborhood was a communal event. *Toledo's* Aug. 13, 1948, headline read "Television a Monoky-Arvai üzletben," the Monoky-Arvai bar now boasts a television. At this point, however, TV was still a novelty. Although television switched public discourse from Hungarian to English, it still brought people in the neighborhood together. Only as television sets appeared in individual homes did its full force begin to be felt. Birmingham's sense of community started to erode. Television replaced grandmothers as baby-sitters, lessening the Hungarian-language link between the generations. Television also provided free entertainment at home, weakening the importance of group activities in the community.

The cumulative result of the war, mobility, and the rise of a television culture was a decline in Hungarian consciousness in Birmingham between 1945 and 1965. This is apparent in the increasing number of English language articles appearing in *Toledo*, the extensive coverage given to campaigns such as Loyalty Day and "I am an American" celebrations, and the Anglicization of many first and last names. Kigyossy's Funeral Home became Kinsey's. Tony

Paczko's Restaurant dropped the z, becoming Tony Packo's. *Toledo* dropped advertisements for the summer Hungarian language school at St. Stephen's Church. In 1948, the only summer notice was for a New York school offering training in "democratic citizenship."

* * * * *

The gradual fading of ethnic consciousness in Birmingham came to a sudden end in 1956 when the Hungarians openly rebelled against Soviet occupation and repression. Hungarian-Americans, who twice in the twentieth century had been characterized as relatives of the enemy, overnight became relatives of the fearless freedom fighters who had defied the Communists and fought for democracy against overwhelming odds.

In Birmingham, self-effacement was replaced by obvious pride. The community pulled together to support the refugees who escaped and made their way to Toledo after the Soviet Union crushed their revolution. The year had a distinct revitalizing effect on Birmingham, even though relatively few Hungarian 56ers settled there.

Community cooperation grew as the newcomers were greeted and efforts were made to settle them in homes and jobs. About three hundred individuals came to Toledo; approximately one-fourth settled in Birmingham. The infusion provided new leaders for the community since a majority of the refugees were well-educated engineers, business people, and professionals.

This transfusion came at an important moment in the neighborhood's history as its economic base was beginning to fail. One after another, the major riverfront industries had closed down. Many of Birmingham's residents were already at retirement age; others were laid off involuntarily as Unitcast, Craig Shipyard, and other major employers closed their doors.

Younger residents were often forced to leave Birmingham for jobs elsewhere. The process was exacerbated by discriminatory "redlining" policies of real estate agencies and banks that were unconcerned about sacrificing

Birmingham for the newly developing suburbs.

Although the new leadership and ethnic pride the 56ers brought with them had significant impact, it was not enough to reverse the overall trend of Birmingham's decline. As the 1960s began, the eventual dissolution of Birmingham as a vital neighborhood became increasingly apparent as the younger generation continued to drift toward the suburbs. In 1962, the Hungarian Reformed Church became the Calvin United Church of Christ. A new era had arrived, the minister said, in which "nationalistic labels were becoming less applicable."

It is possible that, despite the influx of 56ers, Birmingham's slow disappearance might have run its sad course, as the German ethnic enclave in Toledo known as Link's Hill had decades earlier. But in 1974, two events occurred that brought Birmingham back from the brink, both as an ethnic community and as a political force in the city of Toledo.

The first was the proposed closing of the Birmingham branch of the Toledo-Lucas County Library. Residents organized a group called Save Our Library out of the churches and the 20th Ward Democratic Party Club, and, after several reversals, convinced the library board to keep the neighborhood branch open.

The other significant event was an attempt by city and county planners to widen Consaul Street and build an overpass that would have split Birmingham into two parts. St. Stephen's Father Martin Hernady, Nancy Packo, Oscar Kinsey, and other Birmingham civic leaders organized to respond. They mobilized a protest and blocked traffic in front of St. Stephen's along Consaul Street, the main thoroughfare to the Maumee River. Teachers and their students together streamed out of St. Stephen's School, stopping cars and trucks.

These demonstrations, along with sympathetic coverage in *The Blade*, Toledo's major daily newspaper, and some effective lobbying, enabled Birmingham to "beat city hall." In April, Father Hernady, spokesman for the newly formed Birmingham Neighborhood Coalition, addressed Toledo City Council and convinced the members to postpone the Consaul project for ninety days for further study. That summer the issue was voted down unanimously in Council, and *The Blade* trumpeted "Residents Triumphant in Birmingham Area." The bells of all three of Birmingham's churches were rung simultaneously for the first time since the end of World War II.

These two civic successes—the saving of the library and the killing of the overpass—revived Birmingham's sense of community. Furthermore, the energy and political power unleashed by the events had numerous ripple effects, launching the political careers of former Toledo City Council President Peter Ujvagi and two-term County Commissioner Francis Szollosi as well as the formation of the Birmingham Neighborhood Coalition and the East Toledo Community Organization (ETCO).

The Birmingham Ethnic Festival, originally a victory celebration, has become an annual event. Held continually since 1974 on the third Sunday in August, close to St. Stephen's Day, the festival is one of Toledo's best summer ethnic festivals, with proceeds going to Birmingham's self-defense fund.

The 1976 presidential campaign brought Democratic candidate Jimmy Carter to Birmingham, a traditional Democratic Party stronghold, where he and Walter Mondale autographed Tony Packo's Hungarian hot dog buns, one of the restaurant's traditions. Packo's had become part of the national consciousness through frequent mentions by Max Klinger, a character on the popular television show, *M*A*S*H,* who was played by Toledo native Jamie Farr.

In 1976, with a grant from the National Endowment for the Arts, the Birmingham Neighborhood Coalition produced a professional documentary film of the Abauj Betlehemes Christmas folk play. The neighborhood has also been the subject of a video documentary, "Urban Turf and Ethnic Soul," made in 1985 with support from the Ohio Humanities Council. In 1983, the Birmingham Cultural

Center was established by University of Toledo Professor John Ahern, through its Urban Affairs Center. The center has spearheaded numerous projects to collect and preserve the history and culture of the neighborhood, including this book.

* * * * *

The main effect of Birmingham's 1970s revitalization was the rekindling of Birmingham as a cohesive unit. Birmingham was seen not as a random sprawl of streets and houses with a curious past, but a community capable of thinking in terms of "self-defense."

Today, if you drive into Birmingham from the south along Front Street, you cross an overpass and cloverleaf shunting traffic on and off I-280, Toledo's east-west connecting point to Cleveland, Detroit, and Chicago. A large green highway marker hanging over the road, announces, "Welcome to the Birmingham Ethnic Neighborhood."

The sign marks the physical beginning of Birmingham, but the actual community remains larger than the neighborhood itself. Former residents return from the suburbs or across the Maumee River on a regular basis—to buy bread at the Golden Oven bakery, sausage at Takacs' Market or from Calvin United's traditional Hungarian-style sausage made every autumn, winter, and spring, to eat at St. Stephen's chicken paprikash dinners, and to attend church.

In a documentary videotape interview, Mr. Ujvagi, himself a 1956 refugee, noted that there is a large contingent throughout Toledo with an affinity for Birmingham.

"Many people have been surprised," he said, "that we have been able to get people who live far, far away—union leaders, teachers, corporate leaders—to come to the rescue of Birmingham. This is because they still come back, to baptize their children, to bury their dead. They may not live in Birmingham anymore, but there is a life-blood in this community that serves not just the people who physically live in it, but involves people throughout the city."

Perhaps it was the arrival of the 56ers, or the library

and overpass crises of 1974, or both—but whatever the reasons, Birmingham has come to be the most visible and politically powerful ethnic community in Toledo. Writing in his 1975 master's thesis, University of Toledo history student John Hrivnyak commented that "if the Birmingham community suffered from any serious problem in its history, it [was] a lack of political initiative. Birmingham has never had any of its sons or daughters elected to City Council." Ironically, this was written as Birmingham was about to elect both a councilman and a county commissioner. Few Toledoans in 2002 would accuse Birmingham of lacking political clout.

By the time a neighborhood puts up a sign to announce its ethnicity or boasts a large-attendance annual ethnic festival, it may well be that its real period as an ethnic community is over. Tony Packo's pickles, sauces, and sausages are now sold from kiosks in the suburban malls, suitable for mailing around the country. And a book like this one is an attempt to capture the special essence of a time and place that no longer exists.

But visitors still come away agreeing with the residents, the scholars, and the politicians, that Birmingham remains an extraordinary American neighborhood. The European immigrant experience in America, of which the Birmingham story is a core example, is receding into memory. Nostalgia grips those who lived through it, and to an extent, all Americans who have lived contemporaneously with it.

Still nostalgia alone is not enough to keep the immigrant experience from fading. Those with shared experiences and memories of Birmingham's glory days must be encouraged to value and preserve their experiences in every way they can. And scholars who care about the American experience must study and document such places. The results of such studies and preservation form the following sections of *Hungarian American Toledo*.

Birmingham, My Home Town

by William Kertesz

William Kertesz was born and raised in the Birmingham neighborhood to which his Hungarian-born parents had moved in 1915. He had a strong interest in history and historical photography and was responsible for the extensive collection of neighborhood images at the Birmingham Cultural Center.

Before his death in 1996 he gave numerous talks that included the photos here. The information for each picture is in Mr. Kertesz's words.

Looking southeast on Consaul—John Packo's Cafe with front entrance, John Maroda's Bowling Alley, the office of Dr. Louis Marcus, a residence, and the Kroger Store on the corner.

Winter on Consaul Street. Roof of an ice house is in left foreground. Small house on left will be moved and will become 2040 Valentine.

Stefan's Cafe at 1890 Front, in 1936. The building is being prepared for moving, so the High Speed station can expand. Notice the large beams under the building. I sold the News Bee on this corner in 1934 and there was a horse trough there.

Front Street. The Hungarian Brass Band and its director, Gustav Kohler, with Bertok's Building in rear.

Al, a driver for Koerber's Beer. [Unfortunately, we have not been able to determine his last name.]

This picture was taken on or about 1914,on Genesee Street looking toward Bogar street (Ann Street then) with Barones Building on the left. The event could be the dedication of the new church. Note the Malleable stacks in background.

Mr. Stupak was the first man in the neighborhood to own a motorcycle and the first man to lose a leg because of a motorcycle.

The May Coal Co., 2243 Bakewell, in 1926. Left to right, the drivers are Steven "Kinzer" Horvath, Frank Bires, Andy Krizon, "Bones" Csontos, and Steve Hornyak. Mr. and Mrs. Trudeau and office help are in front. The man in the wagon is dressed like a devil. The sign on the truck says, "He'll furnish your coal later, but let May Coal furnish it now."

Red Star Drug Co., Speedy Grill and the Toledo Fire Department's No. 13 engine house, about 1955. Standing in front are Mrs. Fisher and Josephine Egedi. Fireman is Greg Szabo. Man in window is Joe "Quack" Nagy.

This is Mrs. Kardos. She and her husband rented the store as Dan Kardos Groceries in 1926. Afterwards it became Mike Juhasz's, as seen here.

John Toth in his grocery store, 2238 Genesee St., about 1938.

Mr. Joe Jakobs delivered bread for both the National and Birmingham bakeries. The baby in the wagon is Joe Jakobs, Jr., in 1927.

This is 1902 Front Street, Munding's Tin Shop Sheet Metal Works, 1913. From 1913 to 1938, the building had about eleven tenants. Then it was purchased by Tony Packo. The couple are possibly Mr. and Mrs. Munding. Notice corner entrance.

The National Bakery was owned in 1908 by Michael Geyer, who sold it to Steve Toth, who then sold it to Joe Tavcar. Pictured are Mr. and Mrs. Tavcar, their daughter, Mary, and and unidentified person.

The Good Heart Pharmacy, Jo Sziv Patika, 2160 Front St.
Left to right are: Mrs. Serke, Mrs. Fisher, Mrs. Drotar Packo. At one time this was the Humphrey Brothers Confectionery and Post Office Station.

Mr. and Mrs. Gaspar in front of their cafe. Before Mr. Gaspar took over the site, it was Grotar's Saloon.

The Nyitray Brothers Saloon on Consaul Street, across from St. Stephen's School. When the new school was built, beer sales stopped, about 1910. The saloon became Joe Orosz's Sweet Shop and School Supplies, Novelties, Inc. It is now the Golden Basket Bakery.

The Chicago Bargain House, 2052 Front Street. Herman and Margaret Goldner were in business from 1925 to 1956. Prior to this, it was Frank Schramek Grocery and "Bootleg" Store. In 1923, it was Richard Myers Meats. He moved to 300 Whittemore about 1930.

Tony and Joe Galayda. A Four Roses clock and fish dinners are in background. Beer was 10 cents for a 12-ounce glass.

Some of the best cooks in Birmingham: Julie and Margaret Gall, Julie Lajti, Julia Toth, Mrs. Simko, and Anna Juhasz.

Szureti Bal, the Harvest Dance, taken on the steps of St. Stephen's Church. Included in the picture are Mr. Orosz, the butcher, second row, Mr. Julius Rakos on top, Mr. Toth (Harangozo), Mrs. Joe Orosz (candy store), and George Maroda.

"Hungarian gypsies" in front of Monoky's Cafe during Prohibition. Note that the "fiddler" on the right is playing with a pool cue. The group visited hospitals and sang and danced for friends. From left are Mike Buczko, Frank Kerekes, and Latzi Fejes.

The musicians were probably there for the grand opening of the coal year. The musicians are, left to right: Mr. Vargo, unidentified, and Mr. Mescavitz. Andrew Toth sold the coal yard to Mr. Vargo in 1928.

From left, Zatan Halasz, an army recruiter, "Fatty" Kalasz, and John Monoky, standing in front of Monoky's Cafe, 307 Whittemore St., in 1942.

According to people older than me, the neighborhood was ready to party every weekend. This is the lot between the Paragon Station and National Malleable Casting Co. Dan Kardos,the father of Kardy Boray, is third from left.

Mr. John Virag, violinist, at Tony Packo's.

Members of the St. Michael's Greek Catholic Sick and Benefit Society. The organization was the foundation for St. Michael the Archangel Byzantine Catholic Church.

A 56er's Story

By Peter Ujvagi

In 1957, Peter Ujvagi came from Hungary to the United States and then to Toledo under the dramatic circumstances described below. He is chief executive officer of E and C Industries in East Toledo and has served on Toledo's City Council since 1981. A leader in the Lucas County Democratic Party, Mr. Ujvagi served as President of Toledo City Council until his November, 2002, election to the Ohio House of Representatives. The story that follows has been edited from tape-recorded interviews he gave with the editors in April and August, 1999.

* * * * *

I remember a lot about Hungary, my own life and our family life. I remember our escape, the time we spent in a refugee camp, our coming to the United States, and our early time here. I guess I can recall it in such detail because it was so traumatic. I remember my father's business, a small machine shop, before the Communists took it over and nationalized it in 1953. I was just four. Anybody who was a "mussack," a self-employed person, the Communists would just squeeze until they wiped them out. That's what happened to my dad.

My father, Edward B. Ujvagi, was the best of what the free enterprise system is about. When they took his lathes and milling machines away, my dad put together a plastic mold machine in the kitchen of our small apartment. He started to engrave plastic molds to make little plastic BB games. He made soccer BB games and lotto games. He would make them in the kitchen and we all would help. I remember painting the uniforms of the soccer players whatever the popular Hungarian players' colors were.

He also made plastic soldiers. I have three of them to this day. Even after the Communists took his business, my father kept trying to make a better life for us. Those little soldiers are probably my most prized possessions.

In 1956, when the revolution broke out, my dad started making the Hungarian shield, the "koshoot," which has red and white stripes, three mountains, and the cross. He made little pins that the freedom fighters wore. I still have one of those. He would sell these at the "traffics," those little street booths where they sold cigarettes and magazines, toys for kids, and stuff like [the pins].

At the same time he was working at the Gunz factory, on some of the same machines. They took his machines and put them in a factory and he had to work on them there. In Europe, being a machinist or a tool and die maker is a very respected profession. My father would go to work in a shirt and tie and a briefcase. I have pictures of my father and my grandfather, who was also a tool and die maker, standing next to a machine. They've got on white shirts and blue lab coats.

The revolution started when I was in second grade. It broke out in October, so I never finished that year. The school shut down. The year before, in first grade, there was a lot of propaganda. A lot of the kids were becoming Young

Pioneers [the Communist youth organization], so they were getting these nice red bandanas. My parents didn't want me to be a Young Pioneer but I resented that. I liked the idea of marching around with a kerchief.

One thing that changed when the Communists came in was religion class which was taught then in public school. It was still officially available, so when my mother registered us for class, she wanted to register us for Catholic instruction. The principal, a Communist, said he was certain my father wouldn't want us to take it. My dad had to leave work and come to the school to insist that we be permitted to take religion.

There was a lot of pressure on the church under the Communists. That's why I had my First Communion at the age of six. In the Catholic faith you are supposed to be seven years old before you have First Communion. But there was such concern in our parish that religion might be banned that First Communion was moved up.

I remember a lot from those days—there was

[Empress] Maria Theresa's hunting castle on the hill above were we lived. It had been bombed during the Second World War. It was a great place; we use to play hide and seek [there]. It was in ruins so we had all that to play on.

After the Revolution, there were a lot of Russians around because Hungary was occupied. There were a lot of Hungarian Communists, too. But the Russians were the "Iron Fist."

I remember listening to Radio Free Europe. My brother Charlie had very sensitive hands and was able to dial in Radio Free Europe. The government was always trying to block it. We would listen to the news on the radio with the shades drawn and the lights out late at night. I remember the excitement in our apartment building when the Revolution broke out. All the people were talking about it.

But I didn't know what was going on. All I knew were the trucks driving back and forth, because we lived on a major street. Young people [were] running around with Hungarian flags with a hole cut out of the middle. They had cut a hole where the hammer and sickle used to be.

My dad came home late the first night when the demonstrators were going out into the streets of Budapest. The demonstrators gathered at the statue of General Bem, a hero of the Hungarian Revolution of 1848 and a Polish general who had come to the assistance of the Hungarians. There was a big demonstration at that statue and that's really where everything started.

The intellectuals and university folks, writers and such started it. In the beginning, it was a great adventure. And we were winning—the Russians were leaving. People would come to our apartment building with all sorts of newspapers that were being published. I was just a little kid so I didn't know what all of this meant. But everyone seemed thrilled about it.

And then one morning, my parents woke us up in the dark and we saw red lights flashing outside our window. The Russians were beginning to come back in. My parents packed us all up and took us to my uncle's basement apartment down the street. They packed us all in there and the adults put mattresses and plywood against the windows in case there were shots.

We lived in a dangerous place—our apartment building looked down the street where the freedom fighters had established a cannon position. When we looked out our window, we saw a Russian tank aiming past our apartment up the hillside, toward the artillery up the hill. Needless to say, we cleared out pretty fast.

I remember hearing the bombs falling and the tanks by the hundreds coming in as the Russians came back. I remember hearing Imre Nagy, the prime minister, making his plea to the world to save Hungary. I can't say for sure that I heard it directly, but I know that John Foster Dulles was on Radio Free Europe encouraging Hungary to rise and revolt. When we did, we were left holding the bag.

After a couple of days in the basement, we went back to our apartment. The fighting was mostly done. I remember waking up one morning and seeing a tank, a ruined smoking tank, right in front of our window, in the middle of the street. There was a dead soldier lying beside it. It was one of the tanks the Hungarian freedom fighters had liberated from the Russians. It had taken a lot of hits.

We could sit on our little terrace balcony and watch the Russians coming in by the thousands. My parents tell me—I don't really remember saying it—but my parents tell me, once when the Russians were driving by, I said (I had a lisp at that time so they say it with a lisp), "If I only had a hand grenade, I would throw it at them." To this day my mom reminds me of that.

The revolution started on October 23rd and there were about ten or twelve days of freedom where it looked as if we were going to succeed. Then, in early November, the Russians came back. November 3rd, actually. It took them about three days to overcome Budapest.

There continued to be resistance through most of November and into December. A lot of people left as soon as the revolution broke out. Some folks headed straight for the Austrian border but we stayed quite a while. At first my father had no intention of leaving. But when the revolution failed and it was clear that life was going to be pretty miserable for the foreseeable future, he made the decision to go.

We tried two times. The first was on St. Nicholas Day [Dec. 6]. We went in a big truck. My dad had some contacts and he made arrangements for a guide on the Austrian border to take us across. What was like an army truck [was supposed to] pick us up early in the morning. It was still dark out. I was cold and miserable. There were other people in the truck when it pulled up in front of our house. We all climbed in. We had a dog who was sort of a mutt and that dog sat there and watched us as we left. When we got in contact with one of our neighbors a few years later, he told us the dog sat in that spot for weeks, waiting for us to come back.

Once it was clear that the revolution had failed, relief came from the West, from Germany, Austria, and Sweden.

They had white Red Cross trucks set up along the main thoroughfares. The drivers would bring chocolate bars and oranges, and we, the little kids, would come around the trucks and beg. We learned very quickly to say, "bitte schoen, Chocolat"—German for "chocolate, please."

So the truck took us to the railroad station. We got on the packed train heading towards Austria. There was my sister Baba sitting on the little tray you pull out between the seats. Baba was sitting, swinging her legs back and forth. Then she started singing, "bitte schoen, Chocolat."

We were all aghast. But everybody around us smiled. They knew we were heading to Austria. We got to the border and a farmer's house where we stayed for a couple days. One morning he packed us into his horse-drawn wagon. My father sat up in the front with the farmer in this big "bushka," his Hungarian hat. The rest of us were laying down under the straw. This was a great adventure for us kids. My uncle was with us in the straw, so we wouldn't duck our heads up if anyone came around.

That night we started heading across the border—my mom and dad, me and my brothers and sister, my uncle, and some other people the farmer was trying to guide across. By this time they were beginning to reassert some control over the borders. But the Hungarian and Russian soldiers were still out there. They would put two Hungarian soldiers from different companies together so they wouldn't know each other; one wouldn't know if he could trust the other one.

We were walking. We were all walking across these plowed fields, where the Iron Curtain was. The army had plowed the fields to strip everything off so they could watch if anybody tried to escape. Every now and then they would shoot off flares. You could look in both directions and see people falling to the ground whenever the flares went up. You could see hundreds of people trying to make it to the border. We would wait for the flare to die down and then get up and walk along.

We ended up being stopped by two soldiers. The

man who was guiding us and my father tried to separate them and talk them into letting us go. The soldier said he would but he didn't know the other guy. If he let us go, he would get into trouble. So finally they took us in. We were captured at the border and taken to an army camp.

They kept us at the camp for a couple of days in locked railroad cars and then we were shipped back to Budapest where they let us go. They couldn't very well arrest everybody who was leaving. But they had our names and knew who we were. My dad knew we had to leave because eventually there would be retribution.

This was a great sacrifice my parents made. Years go by and I consider what they did—leaving their homeland, leaving a life and family. I'm not sure I could do it. I think the people who did under those circumstances are real heroes. Somehow they were able to just walk into the unknown with a bunch of little kids and nothing in their pockets. All they had was their self-confidence.

We went back to Budapest where my parents made

plans for Christmas. In Hungarian tradition, the Christ Child and angels bring the tree. Saint Nicholas, our Santa Claus, comes early in December but the Christ Child visits on Christmas Eve, so we don't put up the tree until then. The children are told that the angels put it up. My dad bought a tree and put it outside on the outside balcony so everything looked normal.

He was able to make the contacts for a second attempt. But this time it was a little tougher. The people we met were not quite the farmers and salt-of-the-earth peasants who tried to take us over the first time. They were rougher. We had to pay them everything we owned and were able to pull together. My dad had to give his watch to the man who was going to guide us over.

By then it was bitter cold. Two nights before Christmas, we started out walking through the little village. Then we walked across the frozen fields. At one point we walked past an army barracks and had to be very quiet. I can remember looking in the window and seeing the soldiers laughing and playing cards in the warmth as we walked by.

After we had walked for hours, the guide said, "This is as far as I go. You just go in that direction and in a couple of kilometers you'll be in Austria." My father said, "No, I paid you to take us to Austria!" But [the guide] said that was as far as he would go and from there on, we had to make it on our own. He left us many kilometers from the border.

We almost froze on the border that night. We kept walking and walking. At one point we broke through some ice on a creek we were trying to cross. Another time, my father and brother took matches and threw them into a stream to see which direction it was flowing.

Finally we came to a farm house. My mother thought we young kids were going to freeze to death, so she said, "I don't care what's going to happen. I don't care if they arrest us and put us in jail, we've got to stop." My dad banged on the door. The dogs were barking like crazy but they wouldn't open up. Even with the banging and banging, they wouldn't open up. So we kept going.

All of a sudden two soldiers stopped us. My father offered them everything we had left. He had a camera and a few other things in his briefcase. He offered them what little money he had but they wouldn't take it. They said they would let us go for free but they discouraged us from going. Dawn would be coming soon and by now there were Russian soldiers on the border. They said it would be dangerous. But father pressed them and they agreed and let us go.

It was freezing cold. Where it wasn't possible for me to walk, my mother would carry me on her back. Father carried my sister and we just kept going. Sometimes they would stop at the corn shocks in the fields and Dad would try to dig out some of the stalks or some hay so he could put us kids in there to warm up.

In my dad's briefcase were a bottle of rum, a cross they got when my mother and father were married, his micrometer and vernier calipers, the tools of his trade, and a potty for my little sister. We still have everything but the bottle of rum, which they drank on the trip. They even tried to have some of us kids drink it, but we couldn't stand it. I know now that that doesn't work, but they had us drink a few swigs to try to warm us up. They really thought we might freeze to death.

We kept going. We came across railroad tracks and started walking along them. We didn't know if we were heading back into Hungary or towards Austria. We were totally lost at that point. And it was still dark. We came to some kind of control tower. We went into a small building to try to warm up but it was just as cold inside the building as it was outside.

When we were inside, my father lit a match to look around and saw a Hungarian newspaper on the table. I don't remember the name of the newspaper, but it was from a town fairly deep inside Hungary, so he was very disappointed. He thought we had gone in the wrong direction and was thinking of starting to walk in the opposite direction.

We started hearing engines but we didn't know what they were. At first my parents thought they were tanks, but finally decided we would make our way toward the sound and take whatever came. They knew we were going freeze out there if we didn't do something.

We started going along the railroad tracks. My parents were concerned that the towers might have soldiers. All of a sudden we saw a flag on a post that looked like a Red Cross flag. My mother tried to get my brother Charlie to pull it out of the ground. She figured if we carried it, maybe the soldiers wouldn't shoot us. But he wasn't able to pull it loose because the ground was frozen.

Then out of the mist—as strange as it may sound—a man in a trench coat and fedora came walking towards us. My father went up to him and said, "Where are we?" The man said Austria. That flag marked the border and we had crossed at that point. The engine noises weren't tanks but steam engines warming up for their morning run from Nickelsdorf to Vienna. We had crossed over. We had made it.

The man in the trench coat took us to a tavern to warm up. Everybody was exhausted. My mother and father broke down crying. My brother Eddy started playing with the dog in the tavern. We still thought it was this great adventure. They took us to a high school gymnasium where the whole floor was covered with straw mats and other people who had made it out.

Refugees would stay there for a few nights, then be sent to refugee camps. There were notes on bulletin boards from people saying they'd arrived and that if anybody knew their relatives to let them know. My father spotted a couple of people he worked with whose names were up on the wall. They had come out earlier.

We crossed into Austria on Christmas Eve, 1956—December 24th. We spent that Christmas in a gymnasium in a refugee camp. The Red Cross workers gave us oranges, apples, chocolates, and nuts. Our Budapest neighbors knew that we had gone because on Christmas morning, our tree was still on the balcony and not in the living room.

Now this is not an unusual story. Hundreds of thousands of people went through the same thing.

But I'll never forget it.

* * * * *

For six months we lived in various refugee camps, first in Utsaller and Ingst, Kiro, Austria; then, just for a few weeks, outside of Vienna. Ingst and Utsaller are up in the Austrian Alps, right outside of Innsbruck. It was very beautiful but it was also tough. At first we lived dormitory style where everybody slept in rows of beds. The International Red Cross ran the camps. The first American I ever met was a Red Cross worker. They taught us a little English. When I came to the United States, I could say please, thank you, and sing Yankee Doodle Dandy. That was all my English.

We were fortunate because we were sponsored by a New York attorney named Porter Candler, who had the assistance of the National Catholic Welfare Conference. We had escaped the day before Christmas, 1956, and got to America on June 4, 1957.

When we first arrived, we didn't know we were going to Toledo. We came to a refugee center, the old St. George Hotel in Brooklyn, New York, and for two weeks we stayed in one room in that hotel—four kids and my mom and dad. We were basically driving my parents nuts with all of us trying to live in that one room. Then my dad went to the center and said, "I'll go anywhere there's a job." They said, "Well, we have one in Toledo, Ohio." My dad said, "Fine. I'll take it." That was the first time we heard of Toledo. We had to take out a map and looked up where it was.

When we left New York, they put us on the train at Grand Central Station. I remember that we transferred trains in Cleveland at a stop called Terminal Tower. Years later, when I worked at the National Center for Urban Ethnic Affairs, we came to Cleveland to help organize ethnic neighborhoods. We took the subway from the airport and, lo and behold, the subway stop where we got off was Terminal Tower. I stepped out of the subway station and it was like *déja vu*. It brought back memories that were unbelievable. Here I was, back at the rail station I first went through when I was an immigrant to this country, and less than twenty years later I was working for a national organization to help preserve the ethnic diversity of this country and its ethnic neighborhoods.

We changed trains at Terminal Tower and came into Toledo. Father Martin Hernady—who was a young pastor or assistant pastor at St. Stephen's—met us at the railroad station in Toledo, and took us to the St. Vincent de Paul Center on Washington Street.

We stayed there for almost two weeks and my mother thought we had come to the end of the world. For us kids it was a great adventure, but we were in a room next to the room where the men supported by St. Vincent de Paul came to "dry out" after binges. The humidity and the heat were unbelievable. A fundamentalist Baptist church down the street was holding a revival that week, so we had all sorts of new experiences in our first few days in Toledo.

One great part I remember was the basement of St.

Vincent de Paul where all the toys were kept. My brothers and I spent all our time down there. We were in heaven. But two weeks later, we moved into the Hungarian neighborhood. Father Hernady found us an apartment on, of all things, Magyar Street. Magyar, you know, means Hungarian. It was on the street right next to St. Stephen's.

This was in mid-June, so we got to celebrate our first Fourth of July in the Birmingham neighborhood. And except for the time I spent in Washington, D.C., I've lived in Birmingham ever since.

We spent the first summer in Toledo. We spoke very little English, of course, but there were lots of kids in the neighborhood. There were some who knew a little Hungarian, but most kids weren't being taught the language of their parents or grandparents. So we had some real language challenges. But we had a great summer.

There were probably three hundred to three hundred fifty refugees who came to Toledo. And there was a pecking order in our community. The pecking order started with the immigrants and the children of immigrants who came out at the turn of the century; they were at the highest level. Then came the DPs, the displaced persons who came out of World War II. And then came the refugees.

That was us—the 56ers. We were the newest in the community and there was some tension because there were social differences between the groups. A lot of the people who came out in 1956 were professionals, skilled workers, tool and die makers, and machinists. But the first immigrants to Birmingham were mostly from small towns and villages and had farming backgrounds.

My dad got a job almost immediately, I think it was [at] Inshield, as a tool and die maker. He had phenomenal skills. He worked there for a couple of weeks, then one day, he saw the people around him putting all their tools into boxes and closing them up. There was somebody there who spoke Hungarian, so he asked what was going on. It turned out the company had lost a contract and everybody had been laid off, including him. So after only a couple of weeks at Inshield, my dad lost his job.

Then—and this was still in the same summer—another 56er who worked at Jeep Corporation told my dad about Jeep. He went and applied and was hired right away. Before he went, he and my older brother walked from Birmingham out to the Jeep plant on North Cove [Ed. note: a trip of at least five miles each way] to make sure he knew how to get there. He didn't know about bus transportation.

For the first couple of weeks, he actually walked to work, carrying his tools, all the way out to the Jeep plant. By the next April, 1958, my dad had set up a small lathe in the basement of our house and started his machining business. He was also working for Toth Industries on a part-time basis. He would bring work home, work at Jeep and then go in for a couple of hours at Toth and then bring work home after that.

So my dad really had three jobs. Later he moved his machine business into the garage, with a lathe and a milling machine and a small press. In fact, when we celebrated our [E & C Industries] thirtieth anniversary, we took that lathe to have it refurbished. It cost almost two and a half times what he paid for it originally. When he found out, he said, "We're putting it back into production. There won't be any museum pieces in this business." It's still running out there [on the E & C Industries shop floor].

He continued to work two jobs and then eventually expanded the shop where all of his sons—Chuck, Ed, and me—worked. Since I was old enough to reach the machine to clean it, I've been involved in the business. His daughters have helped out as well. Little by little, E and C grew.

Originally he'd made analytical balances in Hungary, precision instruments, but we ended up in tool and die and precision machining. Because of the business, I've been able to be involved in political and social issues over the years.

* * * * *

That fall we started at St. Stephen's School and I went through two and a half grades in a little more than a week! They started me in first grade because I had no language or any other skills at that point. But I spent a good portion of the summer and after school that first year at Margaret and Joe Kish's house. That's where I really began to pick up my English skills.

I spent two days in first grade, then moved to second grade for two more days. I finally landed in the third grade, where I was supposed to be, at the end of the week. I'd only gone through the first grade [and] was in the second grade when the revolution started six weeks after school opened.

We came to the United States in June and by December my father had bought a house. To us that was very important. We were putting down roots, an opportunity that we didn't have in Hungary. We didn't have a car for a number of years. My dad took the bus to work or got rides with friends, because the first thing he wanted to do was put a roof over our heads. I saw some pictures from our first Christmas not too long ago and we all looked so young.

That's it, basically. We grew up in the neighborhood

and we grew up as Americans and made friends. My brothers went to the eighth grade at St. Stephen's and then went on to high school at Waite and Macomber. I went to St. Francis [de Sales High School].

When I was in the eighth grade, I decided I wanted to go to St. Francis, a college prep school. Some people weren't pleased because they thought I should learn a trade. I used to kid that I was the first kid from Birmingham to be bussed out of the neighborhood for school. Except I did it voluntarily! Every morning I got up early, took the Front Street bus downtown, and transferred over.

St. Francis was very important to me and had a lot to do with forming my character. I was involved with the newspaper and edited the yearbook my senior year. I [helped] organize a Young Democrats club at St. Francis my senior year, the first political activity I was ever involved in.

In many ways, I am a textbook example of an immigrant coming to this country and trying to assimilate. Since we spoke Hungarian at home, I kept some of the language.

But I wanted to Americanize. I even wrote my name Peter Alexander Ujvagi because Chandor, my middle name, is Alexander in English. In fact, on my citizenship papers, it's written Peter A. Ujvagi.

And then something happened in 1967, the summer I finished high school. My parents, as a graduation present, scraped together money to send me back to Hungary. Thirteen years later, I went back. It was a searing experience, a really life-changing experience.

For the first time since I was a kid, I heard the Hungarian language spoken on the street. And somehow—seeing the people there, the families, the people I talked to, hearing the language that I was born into, going to church and hearing prayers in Hungarian—re-opened something inside of me. I felt a real respect and appreciation for that.

I really credit my father for my being involved in politics and social issues. No matter how hard and how many hours he worked—and he worked many, many, many hours and I don't know how he did—we always had dinner together every evening. On Sundays, of course, dinner was a big event. Around that dinner table we would talk about current affairs, public affairs, and international issues.

As the youngest boy, I had to talk the loudest to be listened to. I was at the bottom of the food chain! But my father really inculcated in us a sense of responsibility and social obligation, a sense of history, and a need to understand the political happenings in the world.

I was a Vietnam War and environmental activist at the University of Toledo and got involved in organizing the first Earth Day at UT. I was very active but something was missing. One day I picked up Time magazine story about a Catholic priest named Gino Baroni, a Catholic priest who'd been working in Washington, D.C. He was involved in the black community and helped found a credit union and housing development corporation.

He had recently started working with ethnic neighborhoods, the central and eastern Europeans who populated the center cities along with blacks and Hispanics. He understood clearly that people had to work together, that they needed to understand each other, and that not everybody wanted to flee to the suburbs. He knew that when a neighborhood changed, it changed out of fear and panic, and that somehow you had to find common ground between people. He knew the importance of appreciating and recognizing your background, your culture, your ethnicity.

And that rang through me to such a great extent. He talked about the fact that ethnic Americans can be proud of their heritage. Today, that's just taken for granted. Back then it wasn't. We celebrated our ethnicity in our church basements and clubs, but quietly, and not with other people. Because the "melting pot" was still the thing everybody was talking about.

Father Hernady, who had attended a conference organized by Msgr. Baroni in Washington, D.C., [put together] a conference in Toledo and brought together the pastors of all the ethnic parishes in Toledo. He talked about how to preserve neighborhoods, how to address the challenges that were happening, how to stop neighborhoods from being destroyed by everything from redlining to disinvestment to people escaping to the suburbs.

As with everything Father Hernady did, he actually made money on that conference, from the registration fees. Then, over the next year, he used those funds to send me to Washington, D.C., to Msgr. Baroni's second conference. And that's when I really go know Gino directly.

Through Hernady and Baroni, I served on the national board of the Campaign for Human Development, the Catholic Church's anti-poverty program. We tried to take resources we had and to invest them in community organizations that were teaching people how to work and how to fight for their interests and find common ground.

In 1973, I became an assistant field director for the National Center for Urban and Ethnic Affairs. That was a very important part of my life. We worked with ethnic neighborhoods and changing neighborhoods and cities in

Baltimore and Providence, Rhode Island, and Cleveland, Detroit, Chicago, Milwaukee, and St. Louis.

We worked with organizations in those cities, helping them write proposals and develop strategies for neighborhood preservation and for cultural identity. This was the time when [former President Richard] Nixon was deep in the Watergate scandal. My oldest son was born the day Nixon resigned and was baptized the day Nixon was pardoned!

My wife, Betty, moved back to Toledo in 1975 but I commuted back and forth to Washington through 1976. And I continued to work with the Senate for a long time afterward, even after I came back to Toledo.

From my university days, I was very involved in the Democratic Party. Bill Boyle was the executive director of the Democratic Party and ultimately became the party chairman. I consider him one of my mentors and heroes. My father, Msgr. Baroni, and Bill Boyle are the three people who have had the greatest influence on my life.

While I was working in Washington, D.C., Father Hernady got a call from Virginia Clifford, a member of the League of Women Voters in Toledo. She said, "Father, do you know what they're planning to do to your neighborhood?" The city and the county wanted to widen Consaul Street to four lanes and take out Tony Packo's, all the bars on that side of the street, the funeral parlor, two small stores, the VFW, and the Knights of Columbus building. It would have put a four-lane highway through the heart of the community, with the school and the church on one side and most of the residential area on the other.

That was when the Birmingham Neighborhood Coalition got organized. For the first time, all the neighborhood churches came together with many of the social organizations and they packed City Hall. This energized the neighborhood in many ways. A dance group was organized, the sense of ethnic identity became stronger, and a real effort was made to preserve the culture and heritage of the community.

The [next] fight was for the library. The Toledo Lucas County Library Board was going to close four or five libraries because they were too small. The library is such a critical part of our community. To have lost it at that point would have been devastating. I was back in Toledo by then and helped organize Neighborhoods United To Save Libraries. When we were really mad, we used to call it NUTS Libraries.

Neighborhoods United To Save Libraries included people from Birmingham, South Toledo, North Toledo, and the Hispanic, Hungarian, and Polish communities. We had people going into [the branches] and taking out books by the truckload. We increased the library circulation by such dramatic numbers, the three library branches were saved.

After I moved back to Toledo, I got involved again in community organizing, helping to start the Birmingham Neighborhood Coalition and the East Toledo Community Organization. Congressman Lud Ashley sponsored me to the National Commission on Neighborhoods and [former]

President Jimmy Carter appointed me. We focused on how to empower people, how to get people to take control of their lives, their communities, and the future. We finished our report just as the 1980 elections took place. Of course, Carter lost and Ronald Reagan came in. The commission report just sank out of existence, along with a lot of Carter's good ideas.

It took me a long time to decide on the transition from being a community activist to running for public office. I believe that once you become involved in electoral politics and run for public office, you can't go back. It's something that a number of Toledo public officials don't understand, but I really believe it very strongly.

In 1981, when Andy Douglas left City Council to become a judge, I campaigned for the vacancy and was appointed, winning the election that fall. In 1983, I ran for mayor but lost to Donna Owens. In 1985 and 1987, I ran again for City Council and came in first.

Traditionally, the majority-party person who comes

in first becomes vice-mayor, but that didn't quite work with me. I was viewed as a radical at the time and in two instances, deals were cut with the Republicans so I did not get the opportunity to serve as vice-mayor.

Then early in 1989, I decided that, with a city manager form of government, we couldn't really respond to the problems of our community. I would step back until we could change the form of government. John McHugh, Democratic Party chairman, decided to run for mayor and resigned as party chairman. I was elected chairman of the Lucas County Democratic Party and served for almost four years.

During that time, we were able to put the strong mayor proposal in front of the voters and the form of city government changed. I decided that the time was right to make a difference in how our city was going to be governed, to develop a vision for Toledo that was one of strength and enthusiasm and strong neighborhoods and a respect for people, to strengthen the economic base and the jobs in our community, and really bring Toledo back.

And so I decided to run for Council again, now for a four-year term. I ran at-large and came in sixth. I served on Council for four years, then ran for re-election and this time I came in first. This time around, my fellow Council members voted for me and I became President of the Council.

Editors' note: In November, 2002, Mr. Ujvagi was elected to the Ohio House of Representatives, representing District 47.

Church and Community

by Kay Blalock

Economic conditions pushed and pulled the Hungarian emigrant. In most cases, the effect of pull carried more weight. The United States offered economic opportunities unavailable in the homeland. Although most Hungarian emigrants initially planned to return to Hungary, time and circumstances demanded alterations. For many, even a temporary stay in America necessitated the establishment of a church and a familiar social life.

Faith, language, and culture provided the cohesiveness for the emergence of American-Hungarian community; jobs provided the catalyst. As an industrial district grew along the banks of the Maumee River in East Toledo, so, too, did a community called Birmingham.

* * * * *

Throughout most of the 1880s, the site that would become Birmingham remained farmland. William A. Collins, Laura Paine, David Robeson [Robison or Robinson], and F. Valentine owned all but a small portion of this land; contrary to popular histories, the Benedict farm did not fall within the original boundaries of Birmingham.

Three platted communities lay to the northeast: Tredwelldale, Ellenboro, and Ironville—all fated for extinction. On Jan. 10, 1889, William A. Collins, Laura Paine's husband, Henry, and others joined together and platted their property into "lots, streets and alleys, under the name of Birmingham Addition to Toledo, Ohio." A year earlier, they had agreed to the establishment of Front Street and a right-of-way for the Toledo Belt Railway Company, providing the northwest and southeast boundaries of Birmingham. Grand Street (later, Consaul) and the communities to the north mentioned delineated the remaining boundaries.

Despite being inked into the Toledo Title & Trust Company's 1881 map (Toledo Malleable is penciled in), Birmingham's remaining streets would not become realities until 1892: Genesee, Bakewell, Valentine, Caledonia, and Woodford running parallel to Front, beginning from Front Street, while Craig, Paine, and Whittemore run at right angles, beginning from the north.

* * * * *

National Malleable Castings Company became one of Birmingham's first industrial employers. According to the Record of Deeds for Lucas County, Ohio, Alfred A. Pope deeded property along the east side of the Maumee River to the Toledo Malleable Iron Company on Sept. 29, 1890. Five months later, Toledo Malleable transferred the property to the National Malleable Castings Company at a cost of $85,000. This transaction completed a merger begun the previous month; the Toledo operation joined the Indianapolis, Chicago, and Cleveland corporations.

According to a 1943 promotional pamphlet published by the company to recruit office workers, National Malleable had transferred two hundred men to the Toledo location; no date is given. The first year of heavy Hungarian migration to the area was 1892, according to an album commemorating the twenty-fifth birthday celebration of St. Stephen's, the Roman Catholic Magyar Church.

The Hungarian laborers who came to Birmingham in the early 1890s, and those who followed over the next two decades, followed an established pattern. Beginning in the 1880s, Hungarians began leaving their homeland in large numbers. By 1920, two and a half to three million emigrants had migrated to other lands. These numbers included Rumanians, Germans, Croatians, Serbs, and Ruthenians, as well as the Slovaks and Magyars who made up over fifty per cent of emigration figures.

Magyars, sometimes referred to as the true ethnic Hungarians, comprised nearly one-third of the emigrants. Most departed with a specific area in mind, often carrying a name or address of a contact. Numerous Hungarian enclaves developed within American industrial centers, providing a familiar environment for the immigrant factory worker.

Mostly single men with dreams of accumulating enough money to return to Hungary, purchase land, and establish a comfortable life, they moved from place to place in America in search of the best job opportunity. Ohio became one of four states that eighty percent of Hungarian immigrants eventually chose as a final destination, when the reality of circumstances and time made the return to Hungary impractical.

According to Hungarian scholar Julianna Puskas, "No walls divided the communities of various nationalities arriving from Hungary, even in the most closed settlements. The barriers were put up between the new immigrant groups of various nationalities . . . and the communities of the native Americans." This was also true for Birmingham.

Edna Nofzinger grew up in the area that became Birmingham. Her parents ran the Collins estate; her family lived in Judge William Collins' house. She recalled that the foreign people came with the industries. She described the first Hungarians as "aliens . . . the women wore babushkas [head scarves] and the people went barefoot . . . . Our association with them was very limited." She had no memories of any sort of community get-togethers; language differences erected a barrier to such intercourse.

This would change as the American-born children of the Hungarian immigrants began to attend local schools. "Everyone kept to themselves . . . the Hungarian people kept their own customs, from the old country they would say," said Nofzinger. She did remember, however, that the Congregational church she attended as a child shared its building with the Protestant Hungarians until they built a church of their own, a church in which their religion and native language and customs would become intricately interwoven.

* * * * *

The Magyar churches became the major institutions that helped retain the old ways. Following a common American pattern in which early associations primarily existed as classless, non-denominational societies, the earliest Magyar association, the King Matthias Sick and Benevolent Society, included Catholics and Protestants. In 1897, an irreconcilable dispute, reportedly over wearing the cross on association uniforms, split the two groups. The Catholics formed St. Stephen's Roman and Greek Catholic Sick Aid Society. Protestants created the John Calvin Society in the same year. These two associations provided the foundations for the first Magyar churches in Birmingham. According to Puskas:

The social function of the church was important from the start. The Magyar Churches . . . became the centers of social activity much more than they had been in Hungary. The Hungarian church, in many places, constituted the sole 'Magyar territory' that the immigrants could claim as their own, the one place where they felt 'at home,' where they could live according to their customs and national folk traditions. Church services that had some sort of patriotic connotation served to awaken group consciousness and national identity, which is why these parishes celebrated Hungarian national holidays with such ardor . . . . The churches of the Magyars were the connecting links between the old and the new countries, both of which sought contact with the immigrants primarily through their churches.

The churches, along with the benefit societies from which most church organizations developed, provided the familiarity and security lacking in the American city. In the church, the immigrants felt at home with people like them, while rituals and songs performed in their native tongue brought a sense of comfort. They knew that prayers would be understood by the same God who had listened to them in their homeland. Physically, they worshipped in a new land, in America; spiritually, they remained in the world of their ancestors.

In the Magyar churches in America, immigrants "could relieve their souls to persons who felt like them, spoke like them, and faced similar social and personal problems," writes Hungarian-American historian Stephan Bela Vardy. Once established, the Hungarian-American congregations demanded priests and pastors who spoke the Magyar language. And as soon as they could finance their own churches, they did. Until then, they worshipped as best they could in the churches of others.

The Birmingham Catholics worshipped at the German-sponsored Sacred Heart Church, while the Magyar Protestants attended the local Congregational church. Louis Sendi, one of the founders of Birmingham's Hungarian Reformed Church (Magyar Reformatus Egyhaz), now Calvin United Church of Christ, remembered being baptized in the little [Congregational] church on Paine.

As in the old country, the ratio of Catholics to Protestants in Birmingham was about three to one. Despite their religious differences, Birmingham's Magyars joined together in the community's first associated endeavors, as they continue to do today for traditional celebrations. Margaret Brezvai, whose parents moved to the neighborhood at the beginning of the twentieth century, recalled, "although the people had different faiths . . . we were all Hungarians."

Additionally, as social gathering places the churches continued to reflect community (Magyar and non-Magyar) unity through the first two decades of the twentieth century. Mike Dandar, of Czechoslovakian parentage, remembered from his childhood:

> *We had the four churches in the neighborhood: St. Stephen's, Calvin United . . . Holy Rosary [Slovakian] . . . St. Michael's [Byzantine] . . . and there was the black church . . . . I would say that almost one hundred percent belonged to some kind of church, but at least ninety to ninety-five percent went to church on Sundays, which was something you looked forward to because on Sundays you saw other people. You met people who [were] in the neighborhood.*
>
> *That's why I know people from down on one end of the neighborhood to the other end of the neighborhood—coming to the churches and people from this end of the neighborhood going to churches in the other direction. The churches had doings, like chicken dinners, or dances. Usually people from other churches attended the other church's affairs as well as their own.*

As the center of each immigrant's life, the church played many roles. Randall M. Miller and Thomas D. Marzik, in their study of the role of religion on immigrant communities in urban America, stress "the vitality and force of religion as a factor in defining and preserving ethnic life and character in America." The Birmingham churches, each catering to its own cultural group and serving the neighborhood as a whole, defined both community and ethnic identity, as well a preserving the latter.

After the 1897 split between Catholics and Protestants that resulted in the establishment of separate aid societies, both groups made commitments to found local Magyar churches for their own denominations. The Calvin Reformed Society immediately began a fund-raising drive and by the end of 1899, had established a consistory, or governing body, comprising ten members. Having fewer resources than their Catholic neighbors, the Calvins would need nearly four years before they took on the financial responsibility of erecting a church.

According to the church's 1903 cornerstone, eighty-plus members of the community donated at least one dollar toward the church building fund. John Szabo and his wife, Katalin [Szabo Janos es vites Katalin], donated five dollars. Within a year the church was completed. The ups and downs of the history of the church reveal the importance of strong leadership.

Effective leadership contributed to the early success of the Catholics in the growth of their church community. On a Sunday in March, 1898, Catholic aid societies' members gathered and vowed to establish St. Stephen's Catholic Magyar Congregation. Three members contributed the first capital and the group settled on a membership fee of twenty-five cents, to be collected door-to-door.

The Catholics had much better luck retaining dedicated clergy than the Reformed group. They did not face financial difficulties either. Due to their numbers, raising the necessary funds took less time. On New Year's Day, 1899, the Catholics attended Mass in their newly built church building. Before the end of the year, St. Stephen's School opened.

But eight and a half years later, the church, school, and surrounding buildings, including neighboring homes, sat in ruins after a fire destroyed everything but the congregation's will to rebuild as soon as possible. Parishioners attended Holy Rosary, the local Slovak church located at the opposite end of the neighborhood, until builders completed a new church. Large donations from local industries, including $500 from National Malleable Castings Company, helped to complete construction in a timely manner. Dedication of the new buildings occurred before the end of 1907.

The importance of the church transcends religion in the lives of members of ethnic communities. It could be argued that religion and ethnicity are so interwoven that the two cannot be separated. The church and church schools became the stalwart supporters of ethnic language maintenance. God understood the prayers spoken in the native tongue; therefore, it seemed only right that God's servants, both the Catholic and Reformed clergy, should take upon themselves the responsibility of linguistic continuity between the first and succeeding generations.

"The church was to be the link," writes Emil Lengyl, between the immigrants and their American-born children, increasingly exposed to English in the public schools and through social contact with non-Magyar speakers. In church, according to Joshua Fishman, the children "heard the Hungarian tongue, the language of God as the parents understood it. The church was an instrument in keeping . . . [their] children from becoming strangers in the parental house."

Though single men outnumbered families in the early years, the churches never lacked a high level of financial support. With few exceptions, the majority of the earliest Hungarian settlers in Birmingham could be classified as working-poor, and few owned their own homes. In 1900, according to Gregory Zieren's study of property owners among Toledo's working classes, of thirteen nationality groups, Hungarians ranked the lowest in home ownership.

He attributes type of work and small number of families (256:100 male to female ratio) as causes.

An occasional professional owned a home and lived in Birmingham: attorney Stephan Fazekas [Fazekus]; grocer Gabriel Bertock, who lived with boarders above his store on Front Street; painter Julius Bertock; machinist Bela Bertock; clerk, Ida Bertock, and saloon owners who also lived above their businesses such as John Fasztor, John Nagy, the Stephens (father and son), and the Szakovitsz [Szakovics].

Most local residents, however, toiled as common laborers, molders, core makers, rollers, and trimmers for National Malleable. A few, such as Andrew Toth, saw the lack of a future in factory work. They grasped opportunity when it arose and left Malleable to begin their own businesses. As others followed Toth's example in the move from laborer to business owner, patterns of home ownership in the Birmingham neighborhood changed as well.

Although 90 percent of Birmingham immigrants came from a peasant-farmer background, they were neither backward nor illiterate. In fact, statistics indicate that among Hungarian immigrants, 88.6 percent of Magyar-speakers over the age of fourteen could be classified as literate. Craving Magyar-language information and literature, Birmingham's Hungarians subscribed and contributed to a growing Hungarian language press.

They also ensured generational continuity by insisting upon Hungarian-language instruction for their children in church-sponsored schools and programs. And they insisted that their churches retain Magyar-speaking clergy to ensure that the spiritual language of their youth would continue to be the spiritual language of their later years and of that of their descendants. They succeeded. Until the 1930s, Birmingham was a "contained" neighborhood. The Magyar language contributed to this isolation. St. Stephen's School taught Magyar until the 1930s because students' parents requested such instruction.

According to a recent study on the correlation between language and culture, the two are inseparable because language transmits culture, while at the same time it assures the speaker of a place in the community. Although an outsider may become skilled in using the language, he or she always will remain an outsider, to some extent. This connection between language and self-identity resulted in the immigrants' desire to assure its passage to the next generation.

Language maintenance, promoted by the neighborhood Magyar churches, provided unity within the community and continuity between generations. Ella Sundi, born in Birmingham in 1906, recalled that she had to learn her catechism in Hungarian for membership into the early Magyar Reformed Church.

While Hungarian-American children attempted to learn English, a few "Americans" sent their daughters to St. Stephen's Hungarian Summer School to learn Hungarian, the neighborhood language. The interest in language retention may have waned for a time during the early to mid-twentieth century. But the arrival of new immigrants in the late 1950s as well as a renewed interest in ethnicity and one's roots over the past few decades has contributed to a resurgence in language maintenance.

Calvin United Church of Christ Hungarian language classes fill quickly, according to member Marie Wharton. Every Sunday, Calvin United offers a full service in Hungarian as well. Hymns in both languages, depending on the wishes of a family, are available for funeral services. Next to prayer-service hymns such as "Rock of Ages" and "Nearer My God to Thee" can be found Hungarian-language hymns such as: Szivemet Hozzád Emelem, Eltávozott Kedves Halott, and Nincs Már Szivem Félelmére, to name a few. When available, a Hungarian-speaking song reader presides at the gravesite.

Unlike Calvin United, whose membership continues to come mostly from Hungarians and their descendants, St. Stephen's Church, although still considered the Hungarian parish, has adjusted to the changing needs of the community's residents, an increasing number of whom are

Spanish-speaking Catholics. The majority of the Catholic and non-Catholic students in the local parochial school are Hispanic and African-American.

Approximately two-thirds of the church's Hungarian-speaking members and their descendants live outside the parish, according to St. Stephen's resident priest, Father Frank Eckart. Although St. Stephen's choir knows the old Hungarian hymns and an occasional reader comes in, Mass is said in the old language only once a month when the Hungarian-speaking priest from Detroit comes to Birmingham. St. Stephen's works with the Hungarian Club of Toledo located nearby on Paine Avenue and with Calvin United a few blocks away, says Reverend Eckart, in supporting its founders' ethnic customs.

St. Michael the Archangel Byzantine Catholic Church, the last Hungarian ethnic church established in Birmingham, discontinued its Magyar-language services in the mid-1950s. Unlike St. Stephen's and Calvin United, St. Michael's, whose members comprised the lowest number of Hungarians in the community, has lost its ethnic-church quality, according to Father Michael Huszti. After nearly seventy-five years as a Birmingham church, St. Michael's followed its congregation to Oregon, a Toledo suburb. "In doing so," suggests Fishman, "it became another suburban church, with nothing of the old-Hungarian-American atmosphere or orientation."

Besides, commented Father Martin Hernady, former pastor at St. Stephen's, the spirituality that holds the ethnic community together cannot be transferred, adding "American ethnicity must be based on local turf." Hungarian-American identity is defined by place. A West Toledoan who married a Hungarian-raised Birmingham native reiterated this theme when she said, "I have become Hungarian because I live here."

Church and family played an important role in defining community and self-identity. "When you moved out of Birmingham, you moved out of family," said one Birmingham documentary interviewee. The church represents the foundation of the community; it is not just for religious or spiritual needs. It is a "monument built by our parents. Once we let go of the church, there is nothing." The church, according to this speaker, personifies family.

"The church is part of your life," said Nancy Packo Horvath, "part of the family . . . you don't think of the church as being separate from your life." For Louis Sundi, "life revolved around the church," and Pauline LaCacio called the church, "the heart of the community."

Faith, language, and ethnic identity are interwoven to form one of the best representations of Old World community transplanted into an American setting—the Bethlehem plays, or Betlehemes jatek. A European tradition, the various plays enacted in early Birmingham days were versions from different Hungarian villages. [The Betlehemes jatek is discussed in pages 206-234.]

Like other traditions, the plays became part of the Birmingham ethnic identity, representing, like language, a continued heritage belonging to the Hungarian-Americans, the community as a whole, and to each family who made their generational contribution.

Paul Jasco [Yasko] said, "The customs that remain in our family today include the language, the foods, the religious observances, and the proud heritage to be Hungarian." These common identifiers, as ethnographer Daniel Bell calls them, represent ethnicity. Within this tripartite framework of culture, religion (faith), and language, an individual's roles within the community, or social structure, are played out. Weddings, baptisms, and funerals provided different acts in the community life drama.

Weddings, in particular, included signs of ethnic traditions. The Birmingham Cultural Center displays an enlarged copy of a photograph taken at the 1920 Bodak-Weizer wedding and maintains files of others. The groomsmen, who appear in front of the seated wedding couple, carry canes with ribbons attached, and more often as not, they and other wedding party members hold beer (ale) bottles or steins.

In pre-1920 photographs, each member of the wedding party wears a ribbon. This custom followed an Old World tradition. According to Julianna Ludanyi, the best man carried a staff decorated with ribbons and flowers. When Nancy Packo Horvath witnessed such a fellow all dressed up carrying a staff with bells and ribbons, her mother told her," 'that's kind of what they had in Birmingham, too. He'd go on the porch and hit the staff on the floor and make these noises; then he would issue the invitation . . . to the wedding' . . . . I never saw that happen here [in Birmingham], but my mother did," as did the late Anna Galambos Gall and the late Barbara Torok. The ribbon symbolized the personal invitation from a wedding party member.

Other wedding rituals practiced in early Birmingham had Old World beginnings. In Hungary, a wedding party proceeded to the church together. During the reception someone collected money for the privilege of dancing with the bride. After the cook served the last food item, she came from the kitchen with her hand bandaged, supposedly because she burned it while making the gruel, the last dish served at a Hungarian wedding.

Similar scenes occurred in Birmingham. Mary Bence recalled, "my mother told me that . . . the whole wedding would walk to church." Barbara Torok remembered that Mrs. Kovasanski, who worked most wedding receptions "was a real character. She'd wrap her hand in a towel and she'd say, 'How about it? How about a little donation for the cook who scalded her hand?' . . . It was funny, but it was a tradition."

Today, cooks no longer serve gruel or beg for sympathy with their hands wrapped, said Marie Wharton. Reception guests do, however, continue to request a dance with the bride and pay for the granting of the request. Today's groom also grants requests, a dance for a price, to willing female guests.

Father Eckart believes that collecting money for dancing with the bride is an Old World custom of many ethnic groups. The same tradition can be seen at Polish wedding receptions. The ban on Saturday weddings implemented by Monsignor Eordogh reflected an ancient custom, established near the end of the sixteenth century by church proclamation. Although Msgr. Eordogh's ban, it has been suggested, reflected more an unwillingness to compete with hangovers at Sunday Mass than adaptation of an ancient custom.

The church contributed its part to funeral rituals as well. Funeral pictures taken in front of the church show a stopped clock draped in flowers and placed in front of the casket. These photographs included all relatives and close friends of the deceased. A copy would be sent back to the old country. Additionally, mirrors in the deceased's home would be covered. In today's more connected and less superstitious world, such customs are no longer practiced.

Folk art is yet another aspect of ethnic identity. Birmingham's Hungarian pioneers worked hard and likely had little time to pursue traditional folk arts such as dance and embroidery. Continuity between such traditions that have survived from the community's earliest Hungarians and from those reintroduced by newer immigrants remains hard to detect. The art of embroidery appears to have been lost by the 1960s, and dance a decade earlier, although it was resurrected in the 1960s.

Today, forty years later, the arts of folk dance and embroidery have regained strength as representations of ethnic identity. St. Stephen's embroidery group makes a quilt each year and earns money with their annual raffle. At Calvin United Church of Christ, embroidery classes meet two nights a week, Magyar dancers practice on Tuesday nights, language classes are held on Saturdays, and workers still gather in the basement to make kolbasz. Ethnicity remains a family, church, and community affair.

Through combined social-religious events, the Hungarian-Americans in Birmingham maintain an ethnic identity in their everyday lives. Those who moved out of the old neighborhood often return for the holidays, the weddings, the baptisms, the funerals, and for the past-quarter of a century, the annual Birmingham Ethnic Festival, held on the third Sunday in August. Talk to anyone who has ever lived there, and they will say it's a form of self-renewal.

The special occasions, as in the past, are linked to the church. Faith, language, and culture are forever interwoven for those who grew up in Birmingham. The survival of the neighborhood always depended on the churches, and it still does. The ethnic soul of the community is forever connected to the urban turf, and the churches, located on that turf, continue to pump the lifeblood into the neighborhood. Nancy Packo Horvath summed it up best in the community's documentary, *Urban Turf and Ethnic Soul,* when she said, "[Birmingham] is the center of the earth . . . this is home."

* * * * *

The author thanks the people who spoke with her and shared their knowledge of the community and its traditions. A special thanks to Professor Andrew Ludanyi, Department of History and Political Science, Ohio Northern University, Ada, Ohio, who allowed the author access to his video and audio collection, gathered for the making of a community documentary. Material from the Birmingham Cultural Center, written, photographic, and video interviews and transcripts, provided further insight into community life.

Birmingham Folk Narratives

by Thomas E. Barden

Scholars from many disciplines have studied American immigrant groups and the ethnic cultures they developed after their arrival in the United States. Such social theorists and historians as Jack F. Kinton, Richard Kolm, Priscilla Oaks, and Steven Stern have worked in this area. And one thing on which they solidly agree is the importance of folklore to ethnic identity. Much of the research, however, has focused on such public manifestations of folklore as festivals, dances, music, food, and rituals. There has been little work on the more intimate genres such as folk beliefs, remedies, or narratives.

Similarly, most of the work on the folklore of the Birmingham Hungarian neighborhood has focused on the public events such as the Abauj Betlehemes Christmas play, the Sutni cooking ritual, the Corpus Christi procession, and numerous customs associated with church events, including Easter Monday dousings. As important, vital, and fascinating as these folk customs are, they are not the only kinds of folklore to be found in ethnic neighborhoods. An ethnic neighborhood also generates a wealth of folk narratives or stories that circulate by tradition within the community.

I will focus on some of these folktales, legends, jokes, and personal anecdotes that have been field-collected from Birmingham's ethnic residents. Such stories reveal the dynamics of ethnic culture in a way that more public kinds of folklore cannot. Because the narratives come under less public scrutiny as to their correct substance, style, and meaning and carry less formal weight as cultural symbols, they are therefore less static in content and form and more plastic in their potential significance.

Notably, scholars have continued to debate the existence of an American folklore. Alexander Krappe, writing in 1930, stated the extreme version of this position:

There exists no such thing as American folklore, but only

European (or African, or Far Eastern) folklore on the American continent, for the excellent reason that there is no American "folk." The fact is that "folk" cannot be transmitted by colonization and centuries are required for a renewed growth of traditions on the new and hence thoroughly uncongenial soil. American folklore, then, means the folklore imported by Europeans, Africans, and Orientals. There is nothing "American" about it.

This view was based on a concept of the folk, "das Volk," as the lowest economic level of a larger stable society with a long common past in one location. Krappe's extreme theory was a commonly held American and European view of American folklore as late as the 1950s.

Pioneer American folklorists such as Richard Dorson and John A. Lomax did much to put this view of American folklore to rest. Theorizing that a distinctively American lore had developed during the "exploration and colonization, revolution and the establishment of a democratic republic, the westward surge, and the tides of immigration," Dorson held that, even though much old-world folklore continued to exist in the new American society, it was joined by, if not overshadowed by, new genres and forms that were distinctively American.

Work with immigrant and ethnic folk groups has yielded a rich body of collected lore, as well as a body of cultural theory to explicate it. Folklorist Barbara Kirshenblatt-Gimblett, in her study of storytelling in a Toronto Jewish community, named the types of narratives as immigrant, transitional, and ethnic, and suggested this sequence:

1. The immigrant stage is characterized by nostalgia and reverence for old-country narratives for their own sake.

2. The transitional stage typically involves tales of the immigration journey and the new behaviors and values learned from that core experience.

3. The fully ethnic stage is characterized by narratives of inter-cultural conflicts and boundary crossings.

The Birmingham folk narratives strongly support Professor Kirshenblatt-Gimblett's categories. The rarest among the Hungarian ethnic tales in the University of Toledo Folklore Archives are the Category 1, Old World survival narratives. And rarest among these are the old European narratives technically called Märchen, more commonly called fairy tales. These are stories first collected in south Germany by the famous Brothers Grimm and first published in 1812. Only one such narrative has been collected in Birmingham, by David Kovach in October, 1990, from his grandmother, Margaret Kovach.

Once, a long time ago, there was a blacksmith with three sons. Kovach means blacksmith, you know. Anyhow, he had three sons who helped him watch over his farm, the crops, from the top of a hill. They took turns, you know. One day the oldest of the sons was on the hill and this lizard came up to him and asked him for some food and water. The oldest son said no and kicked the lizard until it ran away.

The next day the second son was watching the crops and the lizard came up to him, too, and asked him for some food and some water. He said no too, and kicked at the lizard until it ran away. So the next day the youngest son was taking his turn and the lizard came up to him and asked him for food and water and he said OK and gave him some. The lizard thanked him for his generosity and gave him a gift of three metal rods, one copper, one silver, and one gold. The lizard said the rods were magic and whenever the young man needed help there would be a horse for each rod. All he had to do was stick the rod into the ground and a horse would appear.

Now at the same time all this was going on, the king of this country was trying to find a husband for his daughter. He decided to have some games, so the men of the country could—what's that word, compete?—yes, compete for her. He put a copper apple on top of a really high post and all the men who were trying to win the daughter tried to take it down. But none of them could do it. Oh, I forgot to tell you, they were all wearing armor so nobody could see who anybody was.

Suddenly a man on a copper horse came up and his horse jumped high past the pole and he got the apple. He rode off before they could find out who he was. The king waited for the man to come back, but he didn't, so the king put some silver grapes on the top of the pole and all the men tried to get them down. They tried and tried and they couldn't get at them and then a man on a silver horse rode up and jumped him and got the silver grapes and rode off just like the man on the copper horse.

So finally, the king put a golden bough on the pole and nobody could get it until a man on a great golden horse came and got the golden bough. Just like before, he rode off before anybody could find out who he was. So the king gave up on his games, and the blacksmith's two oldest sons, who had failed at getting the things off the pole, came back home. They had wanted to marry the princess.

When they got back the youngest son teased them and said he'd seen the apple contest from sitting on the fence. This made the brothers mad and they smashed the fence. Then he told them he'd seen the silver grapes contest from up on the chimney and they smashed the chimney. Finally, he told them he'd seen the golden bough contest from the pigpen and they got mad and knocked it down. They ruined the whole place by the time they were done.

Well, then the youngest son stuck his gold rod into the ground and a gold horse came up. And suddenly the son was dressed in gold from head to toe. So he rode back to the king's castle and married the princess. See, he'd been the one in the copper, silver, and gold.

This is a superb version of the Aarne-Thompson Tale Type 577, "The King's Tasks." Field-collected versions have been published in Hungary, Austria, Italy, Slovenia, Greece, Germany, Ireland, and throughout Scandinavia. The lizard as a magic donor is rare, and only appears in Europe in Finnish versions of this tale. The Birmingham version here is the first published instance of the motif from Hungarian or Hungarian American oral tradition.

The next category 1 story is a legend. It was collected from Frank Langel by his grandson, Daniel Kobil, in Birmingham in March, 1981. Unlike the Märchen, legends are believed by their tellers to be true:

Well, look at that man that got killed. This man was a bartender. He had an apron on, you know. And all the men were drinking beer and somebody made a wager—he bets that they would be afraid to go and get the cross from the cemetery, from one of the graves. "No, I'm not afraid!" he said. So they bet him. And he went and got the cross.

Then one guy says, "Now take it back. Let's see if you're brave and able to do that." So the man left his apron on and went and took the cross back to the cemetery. But when he put it back, he stuck it through his apron. Then he got scared, frightened to death. He died there that night. He thought the dead were pulling him down into the grave.

My father always said that story. He swore it happened in his village in Hungary. [The interviewer said, "Well, maybe it was a traditional story."] *No, no, no! It really happened in his village. It really did.*

This is a version of an old and widely distributed European folktale, "Clothing Caught in Graveyard." Although it has been collected in Alabama, Florida, Kentucky, North Carolina, Virginia, and [now] Ohio, it is the kind of folktale Alexander Krappe had in mind when he asserted "there is nothing American about it."

Narratives from category 2, transitional types, focus on the immigrant experience itself. The first example was collected by folklore student Pat Buscani from Ms. Anna Fabos in April, 1985, as part of her work in the University of Toledo's Interdisciplinary Ethnic Toledo Seminar:

Each person had to show a twenty-dollar bill when they got to Ellis Island. This was to take care of their needs so that they wouldn't have to depend on the government. Three of my father's brothers were traveling with my mother, plus one friend was coming, too. My mother only had one twenty-dollar bill between all of them. So my mother stood in line with the twenty-dollar bill and then gave it to my brother and told him to take it to Uncle So-and-So. My uncle kept my brother with him as he went through the line. Then he gave my brother the same twenty-dollar bill and said take it to Uncle So-and-So. That's the way they came out.

This story, it should be noted, does not draw on ancient traditional folk motifs. It is a first-person account of an event that happened during the period of immigration itself. The second example was collected by folklore student Joan Wernert in April, 1987, from Manny Iguali, an Italian-American resident of Birmingham and a custodian at the University of Toledo when he told this story.

When we left Italy in 1915, we got a ship in Palermo. My mother had four of us children. Well, the food was terrible that they gave us on the ship. So this particular day they gave us some broth made out of beef fat and noodles. And they'd always bring some wine with it. So we're sitting on the deck trying to eat the darn stuff. It was terrible. Mother tasted it. "You're right, it is. We can't eat this!"

She said we'd buy some bread, and while we were there there were some little rowboats come around selling oranges and lemons. These fellows were down there shouting their stuff. "Hey, you need lemons, you know, in case you get seasick, lemons will help you." Well, we couldn't afford any of that stuff. Then one of the fellows from the rowboats comes up the ladder and comes up to where we were sitting. Like I said, we couldn't eat the beef or drink the wine either. It was sour, like vinegar.

So we had dumped it all together. We thought as soon as the boat got going we'd dump it over the side. This guy came over to us at the rail and said, "I'm hungry, have you got anything for me to eat?" and Mother said, "No, we don't." And so he says, "Well, what about that stuff there?" And she said, "Oh that, that stuff's no good. The broth was bad and the kids poured the bad wine into it." And he said, "Well, do you mind if I take it?'" And my mother said no.

So that man sat down there and ate, you know, ate every bit of that, that . . . swill! And I thought, oh Lord, I thought we had it bad.

Kirshenblatt-Gimblett's category 3, the ethnic folk narrative itself, typically involves a confrontation or conflict between normative American behavior and that of an ethnic-American giving some active indication of his or her membership in the ethnic group. The following Hungarian-American narrative illustrates this type. Like the graveyard-wager survival, it was collected by Daniel Kobil in March, 1981, from his grandmother, Mary Langel.

There is a custom concerning the "sprinkling" of women on Easter Monday. Men would visit the houses of women and sprinkle them with water, rejuvenating them and imparting good health. Afterwards they were invited in to finish the Easter food and, of course, the liquor. Often the sprinkling turned into dousing. My grandmother told of her friend being dunked in a tub of water while she was wearing her Easter clothes.

On Tuesday, the roles reversed and it was the women's turn to do the sprinkling. Any man, Hungarian or not, was fair game. My grandmother used to mention how there was a foundry in Birmingham with apartments above it. When the men came to work on this particular day, the women in the apartments above would hit them with buckets of water. While the Magyars expected this, the "American guys" who lived in other neighborhoods were surprised, to say the least.

The distinction here between the Magyars and the American guys is interesting because, presumably, both dousers and doused were ordinarily indistinguishable from their fellow citizens. It was the peculiar thing they did that marked them as different or ethnic. Public events such as the Easter dousing were often the way to reveal ethnicity. Conflict, an essential of any good narrative, was often the result.

Another narrative displaying a similar ethnic conflict is a joke I personally collected from Andrew Rakay in May, 1997, at the Birmingham Cultural Center. The joke concerns another ethnic group, the Poles, but according to Mr. Rakay, it enjoyed wide circulation in Birmingham. A non-ethnic police officer attempts to negotiate the linguistic territory of ethnic culture:

One time this Toledo cop was walking his beat and he came up on this horse that was lyin' out stone cold dead in the middle of the street. It must have died of old age or something. Anyhow, he didn't know, wasn't sure what to do about it, so he called up his precinct sergeant on the street phone and said, "Sarge there's a dead horse out here on Kosciusko Street. What do you want me to do about it?"

And the sergeant said, "What street?" And the cop said,

"Kosciusko Street." And the sergeant said, "Spell it." So the cop started out and said, "Kosciusko, K-O-C, no K-O-S-C-U . . . no . . . Sarge, let me go look at the street sign and I'll call you back."

So he was off the phone a few minutes and called back and said, "OK, Sarge, it's K-O-S-C-I-S, no wait a minute, K-O-S-C-I-E-K . . . Sarge, wait a minute, I'm gonna call you back in a few minutes." So the sergeant waited and waited and after about twenty minutes the phone rang in the precinct and it was the cop and he sounded all out of breath and winded and he said, "Hey sarge, there's this dead horse out here on PINE STREET, what do you think we ought to do with it."

These categories then, the immigrant, the transitional, and the ethnic, constitute a basic typology of ethnic folk narratives that pose some interesting questions. What do the stories themselves signify? And how do they work within the group that maintains them over time? Since all of the Toledo material has been collected since 1978 when the University of Toledo Folklore archive was established, and since it was gathered without regard to chronology on the part of either the collectors or informants, there is little that can be said with certainty about the development or devolution of these types.

A rough numerical count, however, reinforces the conventional wisdom that the Old World survival narratives are less important to ethnic groups, while the transitional stories remain somewhat common in their repertoires. The ethnic tales, however, are common.

If this reflects the level of relative importance of the types within most American ethnic groups, including Birmingham's Hungarian population, what does that mean? Stephen Stern, in "Ethnic Folklore and the Folklore of Ethnicity," surveyed the published American ethnic folk narratives and concluded that "overall, the following shifts in ethnic lore emerge: from longer to shorter, from complex to simple, from sacred to secular, from supernatural to realistic, and from communal to individualistic."

The most common reasons he noted for the changes were that much of the content of the older narratives—

magical arts, supernatural beings, and kings and queens—is not applicable to the American scene and that people no longer have the leisure time they once had to narrate such elaborate tales. The newer kinds of narratives, he suggested provide a flexible way to deal with modern American life and the concerns of ethnic groups.

This last observation suggests that such stories provide strategies for dealing with life and social situations. This is a basic assumption of modern folklore theory—that folklore tales educate people in what it means to be a member of a group, validate the group's values, compensate for various social lackings of the group, and help to integrate the individuals into the group. In short, they effect socialization and solidarity. The stories above, from all three categories, do indeed function in these ways.

But I want to suggest another emphasis. The most basic change from category 1, through 2, to 3 in ethnic stories is from the communal to the personal. This shift reflects one of the prevalent ideas scholars have formulated about modern American ethnicity—that in a pluralistic society, ethnicity is not one's fate but a choice. With Hispanics, African-Americans, and Asians, that choice is not always possible because other people may place members of these groups in ethnic categories based on their physical appearance.

But from the individuals' points of view, ethnic affiliation, even in these cases, involves a wide range of personal choices. Communal morés and values that were expressed overtly in the Old World survival and transitional narratives must be reconfigured in the personal experience of each potentially ethnic individual. The community still exists, but it is no longer a given. Community in modern society is an act of will. Stories of contemporary ethnic Americans are assertions of the decision to associate themselves with their group, or their internal conflict about that association.

In his book, *Recent Theories of Narrative,* Wallace Martin has noted that narration, storytelling, has always been a way of establishing and directing behavior, but that modern society tends to privilege biographical and especially autobiographical narratives:

Members of traditional societies, including those of pre-Reformation Europe, patterned their lives on role models provided by their culture. The loss of such transcendent models leads to the idea of selecting a pattern to imitate, rather than having it imposed by the community. This is related to the change from a religious to a secular society and the corresponding multiplication of potential social patterns.

This is an important theme of the new ethnic narrative material found in Birmingham; it demonstrates in story how members of this community negotiate the distance between the group and the individual. It informs us about one set of individuals making the choice to either emphasize or downplay their ethnicity, a choice which has become available to ethnic citizens only recently in the dynamics of American culture.

* * * * *

This essay, written specifically for *Hungarian American Toledo,* makes use of materials from the University of Toledo Folklore Archives. All informants quoted in the article gave written permission for the use of their narratives. Most of the archive materials were collected as assignments in UT folklore or anthropology classes. The author wishes to thank all the student collectors whose work is cited here.

Birmingham Architecture

by Ted Ligibel

From the mid-19th through early-20th century, thousands of people immigrated to northwest Ohio, notably to Toledo. These included French, German, Polish, Irish, Hungarian, Czechoslovakian, Lebanese, Syrian and Greek immigrants who settled here in response to the city's rapid industrialization and the promise of employment. In the 10 years between 1860 and 1870, the city's population jumped from 13,768 to 31,584.

Many of these were German and Irish immigrants but by 1900, the German and Irish populations had stabilized as Polish, Hungarian and Russian émigrés flocked to the city. Ten years later, of the 168,500 residents of the city, 19 percent were foreign born, with thousands more claiming foreign birth for one or more parents.

Prior to the restrictive immigration laws and quotas imposed in the 1920s, Toledo's foreign-born population continued to increase steadily, including the Polish, Hungarian, Greek, Italian and Slovak populations.

By 1920, Toledo's population had reached 243,164, largely as a reflection of the expansion of these ethnic groups. As each new group arrived, elements of Old World culture—customs, traditions, folkways, foodways and other culturally based patterns, including architectural ideologies—were brought to the New World as well.

The various immigrant groups settled in specific, densely populated areas of the city, increasing the potential for ethnic architectural "form giving" or imitating architectural styles common in the old country. Perhaps the most prominent were the magnificent churches that served as the social and cultural focal points in most ethnic neighborhoods.

Toledo churches Saints Peter & Paul Catholic (German), Salem Lutheran (German), St. Patrick's Catholic (Irish), St. Hedwig Catholic (Polish), St. John's Lutheran (German), Magyar Reformed (Hungarian), St. Stephen's

Catholic (Hungarian) and Holy Trinity Greek Orthodox, with their great towers, domes, and spires, readily identified the neighborhoods they served.

Ethnic icons found in statues, stained glass, and carvings were lavished throughout these buildings, both interior and exterior, thereby blending art and architecture. Indeed, it would be impossible to separate church art from church architecture, as the individual elements of the structure, both in form and detail, comprise the unified whole.

Other structures—public halls, commercial buildings, and schools—also featured ethnic-inspired architectural elements such as nationalistic motifs, ethnic insignia and origin-identifying name plaques.

The Birmingham most people recognize is both cultural and architectural. Although many might not recognize the name Birmingham, they would recognize two of its major institutions—Tony Packo's Cafe and the towers of St. Stephen's Roman Catholic Church. Packo's, made internationally famous by actor Jamie Farr—better known as

Corporal Klinger, of television's famous *M*A*S*H* series—is situated at the gateway to Birmingham, the intersection of Front and Consaul streets.

But the great domed towers of St. Stephen's Church provide the visual image with which Birmingham is most readily recognized. The towers soar over the neighborhood and are visible from several vantage points on both sides of the Maumee River. St. Stephen's is just one block east of Front Street, at the corner of Consaul and Genesee streets.

Ethnic-Inspired Architectural Heritage

Over a century has passed since Birmingham was established. In the ensuing decades, the area has grown into its present-day, dense urban neighborhood. The architectural juxtaposition of structures demonstrates its "pre-zoning regulation" period. The perimeter roads, most notably Front Street, originally were lined with shops, taverns, and industries. The largest industries were located between Front Street and the Maumee River, including two of the biggest employers of neighborhood workers—the National Malleable Castings Company and the Toledo Furnace Company, later Interlake Iron Company.

Along the east side of Front Street, a profusion of commercial businesses served the factory workers and their families. Now much of that industrial landscape, including the National Malleable and Toledo Furnace plants, has been demolished, along with entire sections of the commercial development that lined Front Street. In fact, Front Street from Paine Avenue northward has been completely cleared for widening as a primary artery providing access to the Port of Toledo.

During that process, scores of buildings were destroyed, including banks, union halls, taverns, stores, and homes. [Many of these structures were recorded on Ohio Historic Inventory forms just prior to their destruction; the forms are available at the Urban Affairs Center of the University of Toledo.] The interior residential streets are still a dense conglomeration of small-scale, one-and-a-half story homes, interspersed with corner stores, bakeries, churches, taverns, light industry, and buildings of similar "self-sufficient" use.

Construction slowed after World War I, and little new construction in the original neighborhood has occurred since World War II. Birmingham largely escaped the massive post-war public works and urban renewal programs that occurred in other Toledo areas.

Birmingham Terrace, a smaller public housing development, was built on Consaul Street, just east of St. Stephen's School, after the war. Much of turn-of-the-century Birmingham, therefore, remains intact and was listed on the National Register of Historic Places in the mid-1990s.

Birmingham's architecture, an urban architectural tradition, reflects the ethnicity of its resident/builders of Hungarian ancestry. The Hungarian influence is most predominant in three general categories: religious/educational, commercial, and residential structures.

Religious/Educational Structures

Direct ethnic influences in their architecture can be seen in three Birmingham buildings—St. Stephen's Roman Catholic Church, St. Stephen's School, and Calvin United Church of Christ (the former Magyar Reformed Church). As noted, the building with the most identifiable ethnic influence is St. Stephen's Church, established in 1898. The increasing numbers of Hungarian immigrants made a larger church necessary. In 1914, the massive brick structure that stands at the corner of Genesee and Consaul streets was completed.

St. Stephen's Catholic Church

Some architectural elements are immediately recognizable, including the over-size statue of St. Stephen, the first king and patron saint of Hungary that stands in front of the church, and the school's cornerstone, with its inscription in both Hungarian and English.

Cornerstone of St. Stephen's Church

A series of six murals lines the walls of the side aisles; a seventh larger mural is behind the main altar. These murals, along with designs in the stained-glass windows flanking the aisles, depict the lives of Hungarian saints, including St. Stephen, his son St. Emery, St. Ladislaus, St. Elizabeth, and St. Margaret.

Each stained-glass window contains both the old royal coat-of-arms (shield) of Hungary as well as an America shield in the lower panel [page 154]. The shields

St. Stephen's Church
stained glass window

are also placed at the front entry of St. Stephen's School [page 155], juxtaposed with one another. The symbols are important cultural components as well, in that they express the often dual nature of immigrant loyalties in pre-war America, serving as constant reminders of the past and present. Similarly, the cornerstone of St. Stephen's School, cut in both English and

Hungarian royal coat-of-arms (right) and an America shield

St. Stephen's School entrance

Hungarian, is a constant reminder of heritage and ethnicity.

A more subtle form of ethnic inspiration is the design and mass of the church itself, highly influenced by Renaissance motifs, especially obvious when comparing St. Stephen's to major churches in Hungary. Buildings such as the famed St. Elizabeth's Catholic Church in central Budapest, with its classically-inspired facade and opposing towers, are clearly reflected in the design of St. Stephen's in Toledo [page 156].

The architect of St. Stephen's, Toledoan Joseph C. Huber, Jr., won an architectural competition for the design of the church. He described his choice of styles: "The architectural treatment is the Early Christian Basilican with certain features of the churches of northern Italy and of Spain from the early Renaissance; this style of architecture is also widely used in Hungary, where through the past ages it has been adopted as the national church-style." Clearly, even the architect was influenced by the ethnicity of place and chose a style befitting the architectural ideology of St. Stephen's parishioners.

St. Elizabeth's Catholic Church in central Budapest

Calvin United Church of Christ began in 1901 as the Magyar Reformed Church. The church, at the corner of Bakewell and Bogar streets, was designed by Toledo architect, T.W. Matz. Renaissance design, here highly Italian in derivation, was the favored stylistic motif. As with St. Stephen's, the cornerstone is inscribed in Hungarian. When completed in 1905, the church cost $13,000 and could seat 700 to 800 people. The interior stained glass also reflects the church's ethnic composition through its use of the Hungarian coat of arms and the American shield in the same window. The same shields are also found on the interior wall surfaces, painted atop the pilasters just below the ceiling.

Calvin United Church of Christ, 1946 Bakewell St.

Commercial Structures

Commercial structures were built on nearly every block and intersection throughout Birmingham, serving neighborhood needs for dry goods, shoes, tailoring, groceries, legal advice, bakeries, cleaners, butchers, building supplies, taverns, restaurants, and recreational pursuits. As late as 1958, the six-block section of Consaul Street, from Front Street to the railroad, contained twenty commercial structures, including four grocery/confectionery stores, three cleaners, five tavern/restaurants, two bowling alleys, one theater, and three building-supply companies.

The most identifiable ethnic marker is the use of actual surnames on streets and building facades. A number of Birmingham streets have such names, including Bogar, Magyar and Morovan streets. Several prominent commercial buildings feature names associated with Birmingham's founding.

The Juhasz building at 2026 Consaul, the Orosz building at 2126 Consaul [page 159], the Kolibar building, with its unusual paired oriel windows and tiled entry stoop, at 2044 Genesee [page 159], the Richardsonian Romanesque Bertok building at 1920-24 Front St. [page 160], and the Playdium Tavern at 1956-58 Front St. [page 160], all featured facade name plaques. The plaques identify each place as culturally bound to the area's predominant ethnic group.

At top, the Orosz building at 2126 Consaul.

Center, detail of the Orosz building.

At bottom, the Kolibar building, 2044 Genesee, with its unusual paired oriel windows.

The Richardsonian Romanesque Bartok building at 1920-24 Front St.

The Playdium Tavern at 1956-58 Front St.

The most unusual of the several commercial structure is the unique Playdium Tavern. Prominent immigrant John Strick built the Playdium in 1902. A native of Abauj County in northern Hungary, Strick emigrated in 1888, settling first in Cleveland and finally in Toledo seven years later. Keenly interested in the social welfare of his fellow Hungarians, he was an active participant in a variety of religious and secular activities in Cleveland and Toledo.

Hungarians in America describes Strick as "a very generous contributor to the church as well as every other worth-while institution, and his participation in any welfare or cultural movement assured its success." It is not surprising that he built a large hall, originally known as Strick's Hall, to serve the social/cultural needs of his fellow immigrants. Strick's Hall became the secular counterpart to the church. The hall served not only as the major tavern of the neighborhood, but offered recreational amenities as well, including a second floor meeting hall with stage and balcony and a basement bowling alley.

According to Dr. Andrew Ludanyi, professor of history at Ohio Northern University and an authority on Hungarian culture in the New World, the very design and pale yellow brick color have direct, Old World Magyar antecedents. Indeed, the graceful arches with quoined surrounds on the second floor and the heavily Renaissance-inspired cornice are hallmarks of many public and religious structures in Hungary.

Close inspection, however, reveals the most remarkable aspect of Strick's Hall—that of its fantastic array of Hungarian ethnic symbols situated within the deteriorating tin cornice at the building's roofline. Here, among Renaissance-inspired parapets and dormers, are the most revered symbols of Hungarian culture—the national coat-of-arms, the crown of St. Stephen, and the Hungarian cross.

Detail from the Playdium Tavern, formerly Strick's Hall, the national coat-of-arms, the crown of St. Stephen, and the Hungarian cross

The coat-of-arms dominates the central dormer on the

Front Street facade, and features a shield which incorporates the flag of Hungary with the Hungarian cross. Atop the shield is the crown of St. Stephen with its characteristic bent cross. Similarly, small cartouches located just below the cornice and dividing the window bays, feature the Hungarian cross at the center.

Detail from the Playdium Tavern,
cartouche with Hungarian cross at the center

The impact of ethnicity as a "form giver" is nowhere more culturally-determined and evident than in this important building. And although this structure was probably architect-designed, there is no better example of ethnic-influenced vernacular architecture on a secular building in the area. Toledo architect David L. Stine, designer of the Lucas County Courthouse, the county jail and sheriff's residence, and Libby House, is believed to be the architect of Strick's Hall. Stine designed Strick's summer home on Lake Erie, hence the obvious connection.

Residential Structures

The homes of Birmingham are mostly modest, one-and-a-half story dwellings. About seventy-five percent are frame construction with twenty-five percent built of brick. Almost exclusively, the homes have gable fronts, with two

One-and-a-half story homes in Birmingham

windows and a door facing the street. Sometimes the door is centered, but more often it is offset, making the facade asymmetrical.

A 1907 *Toledo Blade* article described the homes:

Their homes are, as a rule, in [sic] cheaply built, one-story cottages, but, as an evidence of thrift. It is asserted that 250 of them are absolutely owned, or are being bought on the small payment plan by their occupants. The cottages are usually on small lots, many of them fronting unpaved and bottomless mud streets, in close proximity to the smoke belching factory chimneys. A few of the more industrious Magyars, who have had the advantage of several years' residence here, own two such cottages, occupying one and renting the other for $7 to $9 a month to some less fortunate countrymen.

Most of those cottages still exist, although the belching chimneys and unpaved streets no longer plague the neighborhood.

Fences were important in defining property boundaries. Elaborate iron fences surrounded dozens of homes, even though they were on very small lots. Small plaques in the center of the gates reveal that the fences were cast by the T. Stewart Company of Cincinnati. Why so many were

Elaborate iron fences line many Birmingham streets

cast in Cincinnati and shipped to Birmingham is unknown.

Many of these fences, or their modern chain-link counterparts, remain today, giving Birmingham the highest proportion of yard fences in the city. Perhaps this was an expression of possession, a comment on the newfound right to own property. Many of Toledo's immigrants were tenant farmers in Hungary and owned no land, coming primarily from the poor agricultural region of northeastern Hungary . . . the counties of Abauj, Heves, Zemplen, and Gomor.

When the immigrants began to build homes, they

logically chose a type that was not foreign but was also acceptable in their new environment. In this way they were able to retain certain cultural ties to their homeland. According to *Hungarians in America*, "The first immigrant families settled in Toledo in 1891. Around the 'Old Factory,' [National Malleable Castings Co.] soon a veritable little Hungarian village grew, consisting of characteristic Hungarian rural homes." Distinct similarities can be found by comparing Toledo's Magyar Street with a street in the rural

At top, Magyar Street in Toledo. At bottom, Atany, in northern Heves County, Hungary

Hungarian village of Atany in northern Heves County.

The size, scale, setback, roof type, fenestration, and placement are strikingly alike. The unusual arrangement of houses on Magyar Street—two homes side by side with an open space in between—is found in Atany as well. This arrangement reflects the importance of yards in Hungarian village life, as noted in *Proper Peasants*: "Most domestic activities are performed in the living room in winter and in the kitchen or the yard in summer . . . like boiling soap, making plum jam, drying fruit, rendering fat, pig sticking, and cooking for the festive meals are all done outside." Such residential grouping is not accidental, but is a subtle example of Old World, ethnic-based "form giving."

The most extraordinary parallel between the homes of Toledo and those in the northern Hungarian counties can be seen in a unique architectural form with no known antecedent in Toledo. This is the double-rounded arch found on five homes in Birmingham, four of which are on Whittemore Street. This unusual arrangement consists of two oversized archways, serving as a corner entry.

The main arch is on the facade and in three cases is a flattened, basket-handle shape; the other two are typical round arches. The side-facing arch is round-arched in all five instances. These homes are found at 222 Whittemore, 318 Whittemore (now obscured), 402 Whittemore and 404 Whittemore and at 2143 Bakewell [page 170].

At top, 222 Whittemore. At bottom, 402 and 404 Whittemore Street.

2143 Bakewell St.

Round and flattened arches are found throughout Hungary, Czechoslovakia, Poland, Romania, and Austria, in some medieval homes in Budapest, many rural houses near the Austrian and Czechoslovakian borders, and on a Balatonakali farmhouse in Central Hungary.

Rounded arches on Balatonakali farmhouse

These arches echo both earlier Romanesque forms and the prolific resurgence of the arch during the Renaissance. Round-arched motifs were preferred for both urban and rural, high style and vernacular, and domestic and public structures from the 1600s onward in Hungary.

Similar archways are found on homes in rural northern Hungary and on a larger scale throughout the country. Traditional house design is described in *Proper Peasants*:

Houses at Atany are one-story buildings, like those of other Hungarian villages. The walls are constructed of adobe and the roofs are thatched with reeds. Traditionally these houses consist of three or four rooms: a living room (which is also used for sleeping), a kitchen, a pantry, and a loft above. Usually one end of the building faces the street. The rooms are arranged linearly with the living room, "the House," at the street end and the pantry at the other end with the kitchen in between. Many houses have a veranda on the entrance side of the building; thus people do not enter directly from the yard but through the veranda. From the veranda (or from the yard if there is no veranda) one enters the kitchen.

With only minor changes, this depiction of a Atany

house could well be that of a house in Birmingham. The major attributes are virtually the same—one-story with a loft (our one-and-a-half story), adobe construction (our brick), street-facing gable, an entrance veranda, the living room at the street end, and primary entry into a room other than the living room.

The few changes include roofing material, entry into the dining or a family room (now) and larger veranda archways, with only two arches or openings at the immediate corner of the house rather than an arcade extending down the side. In the New World, the Atany kitchen has become the dining room; the pantry becomes the kitchen. Fences are also common in Atany, but are often made of vertical sticks placed very close together.

Ethnic tradition has played a major role in giving form to Birmingham's architectural heritage, as well as its broader cultural context. Examples of this ethnicity include, as Professor Ludanyi notes, "complex systems of mutual support linked directly to the neighborhood's cultural heritage . . . family and friendship ties . . . the personal concerns of a single person become those of many . . . neatly kept streets or [in] the numerous gardens . . . intricate embroidery that decorates the interiors of many local homes . . . preparation of traditional Hungarian foods . . . holidays celebrated in honor and respect for one's ancestors . . . each church continues to hold Hungarian services . . . a Hungarian dance troupe . . . in both Byzantine Catholic and the Hungarian Catholic churches, a Christmas mummers play —hundreds of years old and brought over by the original immigrants—is performed each year . . . the annual local ethnic festival."

Other physical evidence of ethnic influence can be seen in the neighborhood as well—the whitewashed trees lining the 1800 block of Genesee Street, used as the processional route during the feast of Corpus Christi in October or the bas relief statues of Hungarian saints on the rear wall of the more recent addition to St. Stephen's School.

Architecture can be added to these ethnically inspired cultural legacies and traditions. Birmingham's churches, schools, businesses, and homes are a reflection of Old World architectural customs—a heritage transformed to conform to accepted American norms, yet retaining ethnic identity through form, color, design, detail, and placement. The architectural heritage of Birmingham is one of Toledo's most important cultural treasures representing an urban architectural legacy of extraordinary measure.

Recipes and Ethnic Identity

by Lynn Hamer

We learned how to bake these Hungarian cookies from our mothers. Now we are teaching our daughters and our daughters are making their own, so we don't have to worry about baking for them. Before this, we were always having to worry. We had to bake two, three batches because we needed them for our daughters, for their families. So now they are making their own—and they bake for me now.—Ann Mascsak, St Stephen's Church, Feb. 16, 1998

* * * * *

It was important to collect these recipes because a lot of our older people were dying out, and some of the young people just didn't keep their recipes. This is one of my main interests: that these recipes will be salvaged and continued with the family. For instance, I know when we do our baking for people that would like to buy the baked goods down at Calvin United Church for Easter or Christmas, we have young people that walk in and they say,

"Oh, this smells like my mother's kitchen!" And we say, "Okay, will you continue this?" Or, "Do you have the recipes?" Or, "When we're gone are you going to be able to take over and do this baking for your children and grandchildren?" Many of them say they don't even have the recipes!—Judy Balogh, Calvin United Church, March 31, 1998

* * * * *

You have to remember, this Easter baking day doesn't just happen; it comes from the time you are raised in this atmosphere of giving of yourself. I think that is one of the secrets. The reason we are doing this baking is it really makes you feel like you are doing something useful. First of all, you meet a lot of wonderful people and you make friends that way. Just to stay isolated in your own home and just to do family things, to me, it isn't enough. I think that is why these people are here today—and we do have some of the younger ones now, for which I am glad . . . because I used to worry, "Oh my goodness, what is going to happen?" But the younger ones have the recipes, and they know what to do.—Agnes McDaniel, Holy Rosary Church, April 4, 1998.

* * * * *

The cliche "you are what you eat" takes on significant meaning when considered in the context of how people inherit, learn, and create a sense of their family, ethnic identity and community. Family practices, such as baking and eating, provide the first and often deepest source of ethnic identity, while group practices, such as collecting recipes and holding church baking days as fundraisers, extend ethnic identity to a larger group.

Ethnicity can refer to both religious affiliation and national origins. Although belonging to an ethnic group sometimes is based on physical appearance, location of home, language or accent, or name, the decision to establish and maintain identity with an ethnic group is often a matter of choice and participation—less a static matter of birthright or "blood" than a dynamic, intentional process of becoming part of a community whose members identify with each other as all sharing an important bond.

The practice of making compiled cookbooks or

fundraising cookbooks emerged during the Civil War and has remained popular ever since. This section draws on printed recipe collections from Calvin United, Holy Rosary, and St. Stephen's churches and the Birmingham Cultural Center, as well as interviews and observations conducted in the spring of 1998 with women involved in baking events in the churches.

Both the baking days and the compiled cookbooks exist because of the need to raise funds to support churches and their schools. The participants share a strong aesthetic standard. Comparing homemade or church-made pastry to commercial products, Ann Mascsak said, "The texture is quite different . . . . You know my mother's kalacs used to be so nice and moist and what they make now, what they make in the bakery, is just dry."

Going "beyond necessity," bakers brush Hungarian nut rolls with egg yolk before baking, to give the finished product a shine; they decorate Slovak tea cakes with frosting, nuts, and candied cherries, and, as Sue Pohlman said, many consider their baking to be an art form:

You are creating it, you are designing it, you are even presenting it. When I do the Dobos Torta, I don't put the layers together and slap frosting on the top; I pipe frosting along it, and put on the finishing touches. So, you know, in a way, you add your own personal touches to it, just like you would a painting.

Learning through Social Interaction

As children, most of the women interviewed watched their mothers, grandmothers, aunts, in-laws, and neighbors cook and bake. Lillian Keil recalled:

When I was a child, and I was very much interested in [baking] *and wanted to help her* [my mother], *but she'd tell me, "No, your hands are dirty, you can't." And I remember going to the bathroom and washing my hands and telling her, "See Mom, it's clean." She'd say—she had no patience—she said, "Go see your father."*

So my father was always busy in the outdoors, and I remember him putting me into turning the honing deal where he was sharpening knives. And then I was a go-fer for him. He'd say, "Go get me the screwdriver, go get me the wrench." So I learned the tools of a man's trade, which comes in handy because I know what tools I need for whatever repair jobs.

I probably was a small child when my mother started letting me help, but then all I was allowed to do was to put the nut filling in. Of course, she put me in to grinding the nuts. At that time we had the shelled nuts . . . . I loved nuts . . . and I would probably eat more. She would scold me, she'd say, "I'm not going to have enough for the filling [because] you keep eating them!"

Lillian's mother let her child do tasks that were easy and easily corrected. Similarly, when a new person came to a baking day at the church, the seasoned bakers started her or him out "running"—delivering the dough, filling, and tools to the more experienced participants who actually did the rolling, cutting, filling, and shaping.

People participate in many overlapping communities, each of which provides different experiences and expertise. When asked how she learned to bake, Virginia Molnar said:

I probably learned the most coming here to help because I was always afraid of working with yeast dough. I remember at home I couldn't run through the house. You couldn't go in the kitchen because the dough was rising. Then when we came down here, we learned how to make those rolls. So I really learned a lot—not that my grandmother and my mother didn't bake, but when you are a child, you just kind of help out with the little things and you don't actually do the whole process. But once I came down here, I wasn't afraid to try it on my own.

The necessity of such apprenticeship over time is clearly appreciated. Anne Walko, whose mother was an active Holy Rosary baker, explained how she came to that position:

My mother said, "Well come and help us!" They [her contemporaries] *were getting older and we kind of took over. While they were still here they would tell us what we were doing wrong.*

Similarly, Anne's niece, Katherine Galatocky, explained how she had been recruited to learn, through apprenticeship, to lead a next generation of church bakers:

I had to be there this morning when she [Aunt Anne] *felt the dough and it was too sticky. Then we had another batch that we were doing, it was too sticky. I knew that it was too sticky, and I said, "What do we do here?" It was all ready to be cut into the cookies. She said, "Oh just add a little flour to it," which I wouldn't have thought about. Then* [with] *the next dough, which was right, I could tell the difference. That is what I am learning, those different things. And when she is not here, boy is that going to be something.*

Novices learn skills and knowledge over time with essential feedback from experts. At the same time, a more subtle learning occurs as the novices come to feel they, too, are part of the community made up of the older and more expert members. Judy Balogh emphasized the emotional component of learning a skill by practicing it within a close community, her family.

I always loved to work with my mother when she made the strudel . . . . That was just on certain occasions, because we were always so busy on the farm. But every now and then we would get so hungry for strudel, and my mother would make up this dough. She would prepare the dining room table with a big white table cloth, and she would put this dough in the middle of the table cloth and she'd say, "OK now, we are going to start stretching this."

And we had to take our rings off of our fingers, and we couldn't have long fingernails, and we used the back of our hand to stretch [the dough]. *We couldn't wait until the* [the dough] *was all spread out on the table. Then it had to dry, and then she sprinkled it with the melted butter—we always had butter on the farm.*

And we didn't have apples down south [in Louisiana] *at that time, so we used the cabbage. That was one of our favorite, made with cabbage. But we had to be very careful when we stretched the dough so we didn't make a hole in it. And we would go round and round the table, and we kept stretching it, and it was so much fun, working together.*

Those are some of the memories I have of working with my mother. And you don't forget it, when you work with you mother and prepare these recipes. It sticks with you, because it's such a special thing when you do it with your mother. . . . It's that closeness.

* * * * *

The intimacy of participation seems essential to the mastery of the skill, and memory of the specific lessons is enhanced by emotional bonds. Similarly, the communal, affective aspect of learning to bake occurs within the church group. When asked how she learned to bake, Marge Juhafc said:

I learned to bake down here with the ladies. They were wonderful. Anna May and Rosemary, their mom, and both the aunts worked down here. What we didn't know, they showed us. What I didn't learn at home from my mother, I learned over here. It was really great. In fact, they even opened their homes and we went there. We wanted to make the nut and poppy seed rolls, but we didn't know how to start.

They showed us from the beginning of getting your flour—everything. Because you read a recipe in a book, but you have got to know how to put it together. And that is the most important thing . . . . They were just like family to me. Everybody knows everybody else who knows everybody's family.

In Marge's account, specific skills like choosing one's flour are given less emphasis than the social aspects of going to the experts' homes and coming to know and work with them closely—"like family."

Important aspects of baking are learned through observation and apprenticeship. The best cooks and bakers from earlier generations neither measured ingredients nor used recipes. Virginia Molnar said:

The older people [who] *used to make the nut rolls, they didn't have a recipe. If you asked them how to do it, they would say, "A handful of this, a handful of that." I remember when I* [got] *married and I wanted to learn how to make those nut rolls, I went over to my aunt's. And she said, "If you just come over one day, I am going to* [make them]*." She threw everything into the bowl and said, "This needs a little more sugar—it is not rich enough." She took the cream, took the butter and just dumped* *them in there and just mixed it up. "OK now, put your hands in here and feel how this is supposed to feel."*

Even when they were written down, recipes alone were not sufficient. As Marge Juhafc said of her mother's recipes, "She wrote everything down but she didn't tell you how to do it."

Writing and Using Recipes

Written recipes are an important part of traditional practice. These recipes not only serve as guides that help the bakers remain true to the long-established standards, but when collected, the recipes can be printed and sold as fundraiser cookbooks. Written recipes can include informal documents, written on notebook paper and intended for personal use or use within the church group; more formal, typed and xeroxed booklets intended for distribution to those interested in maintaining or reviving baking traditions, and formal, printed books intended for sale.

As Agnes McDaniel remembered, younger participants have long seen written recipes as essential to their being able to continue the traditions of baking at home or at church. She recalled writing down recipes based on observations at home and at church:

I remember going over to my mother's house. I lived almost across the street from my mother after I got married and I would help her. I would say, "Ma, how much flour do you use for this?"

"Oh, just a sifter-full."

I measured to see how many cups there were in a sifter and said, "I'm coming over one day and I am going to sit there and I am going to write down everything you put in that dough."

She said, "OK."

Since that time, I passed this recipe on to my sister-in-law, my sisters, and my daughter in California—and she passed it on to her daughter. We make it out of twelve cups of flour. It never fails; it is always good.

I started baking for the church many years ago, when my mother, my aunt, and Mrs. Anna Bacho, Mrs. Helen Beres, Mrs.

Elizabeth Sinay, and Mrs. Appolonia Kralovic were all baking in the old hall, which was originally Holy Rosary Church. They were good bakers. And they were very serious about what they did. That is how I got started and how I think some of the other ladies got started. During that period, I was the only younger woman there.

These recipes we are using have been passed down from way way back. You see, the ladies really didn't have a recipe —so many sifters of flour and so much butter and shortening and yeast. This is how they did it. So some of us took it upon ourselves to write them down, and that is how we got them.

The raised dough recipe is the same because Mrs. Walko has kept it. If we changed anything, we would insert it in the recipe, if we thought it was better.

As Agnes McDaniel described, writing recipes while observing skilled cooks and bakers was and is common practice at home as well as at church. Margaret Hayden's son, Steven, has written down several of her recipes, including her soup recipe, and she has added her own notes to his, trying to communicate in writing what would usually be observed.

During her high school days, Shannon McDaniel Maza, Agnes McDaniel's granddaughter, regularly went to her grandmother's house for cooking lessons. Shannon wrote down most of Agnes's special recipes in what they called the Black Book; later, Shannon typed the recipes in a computer and printed *Grandma's Secret Recipes* for the family.

Similar to family collections, community collections ranging from informal to formal are occasionally created and distributed. One collection was made in 1994 by the Birmingham Cultural Center. As Judy Balogh explained:

> *We decided that we would have a program, and each person would bring their recipe and we'd make it into a book. And each person would bring a sample of what they baked. . . . It was a tremendous turnout, with fantastic interest.*

For this collection, the bakers themselves brought their recipes, some of which appear to have been revised for a less-experienced audience, as many include quite detailed instructions for preparation.

At other times, written recipes have been created, based on practice, explicitly for fundraising cookbooks. Grace Molnar contributed a potato pancake recipe to the St. Stephen's Mother's Club cookbook. She "had it memorized, and just wrote down the recipe and the directions."

While writing down recipes is important, knowing how to use the written recipes is equally vital. As the emphasis placed on observing and practicing with skilled bakers suggests, reading a written recipe is not enough to learn how to cook or bake well. Lillian Keil spoke about a friend who relied on the printed recipe alone, explaining why the knowledge of feel, learn-through-observation, and apprenticeship is necessary to successfully bake butter cookies from a printed recipe:

It is very difficult to follow the cookbook recipe in the cookbook that St. Stephen's has because they are assuming you know how. But when you mix these butter cakes, you have to use your hands. You put your butter in with the flour. And you keep working with your fingers until it is a little yellowish color before you put in your eggs and your sour cream.

When I worked at Internal Revenue, one of my coworkers was crazy about my cookies and asked for the recipe. I gave her the cookbook and she tried the Hungarian pastry. Then she invited me over the Christmas holidays and gave me one of the cookies. I almost broke my tooth! I said, "Ruthie! What did you do?"

And she said, "I mixed it just —"

I said, "By the way did you mix it on the mixer?"

"Well yes, just like any other cookie."

I said, "You can't do that. You have to do it by hand."

[You don't get] *the flaky texture if you do it in the mixer. It has to be done by your hand so you feel the texture of that dough.*

Each time the dough is mixed, the recipe may need to be revised, depending on the brand or quality of the ingredients, the weather, or other factors. Virginia Molnar, who with her sister, Anna May Zajcz, has been responsible for mixing the dough for St. Stephen's baking days, said:

I do have a recipe [for the butter cookie dough], *but you do not always follow it. I remember when Julia Toth used to be cooking down here. She would mix it up and roll the dough out and say, "Oh this isn't rich enough! You know the butter is different nowadays."*

I always used to snicker to myself . . . flour is flour and butter is butter. But what she said is true. My sister and I were talking about it yesterday. It does make a difference as to what kind of ingredients and you do have to make adjustments sometimes, [if] *it is either two dry or too rich.*

Finally, as Lillian's story about the failed butter cookies suggests, as people practice making recipes from cookbooks, the responses they get from their audiences, those who eat the products, tell whether or not the bakers are successful and therefore how expert they have come to be.

Those recognized as good bakers receive praise for their work—usually requests to make the recipe again and again. Through practice, such recognized experts develop their own variations on the written recipe. Notes can be added in the margins of the individual's cookbook; sometimes they are simply remembered. When asked if she uses her church's cookbook, Virginia Molnar said:

> *I make a cottage cheese cake out of there all the time, Mrs. Fabian's recipe. And when I make it people say, "Oh, can I have the recipe?" I say, "It's in the cookbook, and these are the revisions." So I do use it. If it is in there, how to do it, I will look it up for reference.*

Recipes are written down, but they can be insufficient if used alone, without observing and working with master bakers. Although the recipe may at first appear to be a standardization of a practice, which would lead to products becoming more uniform from person to person and from group to group, in actual use, little standardization occurs, since individuals are constantly adjusting and improving upon the recipe.

Conclusions

Group baking and written recipes are links to the

symbolic root of ethnicity—the old country. Grace Molnar, whose parents came from Hungary, said, "All the recipes that we all make now actually came from Hungary." The practices of making and serving food are seen as continuous with those in the old country. Sue Pohlman explained:

Hungarians are fun-loving people, and that's how you can share something of yourself . . . by cooking. When we went to Hungary, the first thing they offer you is something to drink, something to eat. . . . I guess it's like gifts from the heart.

The recipe collections are symbolic of the transition from Hungarian to Hungarian-American. This is most explicitly stated in the St. Stephen's cookbook index:

Besides the treasured recipes of their native country, Hungarian Mothers have adopted many American recipes and adapted them to their Hungarian style of cookery. Our cookbook contains a complete section of these Hungarian-American favorites.

Such Hungarian-American recipes include Spaghetti Supreme, Sweet Potato Puff Casserole, Malted Milk

Cake, and English Drop Cookies. Folklorists Yvonne and William Lockwood have noted that the melting pot model of cultural diversity, while flawed in many respects, remains useful in considering culture as represented in a concrete way in food and foodways that are easily borrowed and adapted from one group to another.

Folklorist Barre Toelken notes that performers of traditions make changes or innovations, but "within the framework of the familiar, acceptable, and culturally logical."Thus some foods are adopted (Judy Balogh's Louisiana family added baked sweet potatoes to their menus), but some are not (Judy's family ate fried fish, as had been prepared in Hungary, but never baked fish or shellfish, both popular among their neighbors). Similarly, when asked if the nut and poppyseed rolls are originally Slovak, Agnes McDaniel explained:

Oh yes—well, as far as I know. Who knows? They might have borrowed from one another for all I know. We were next-door neighbors to Hungarian people, and my mother learned to make things that the Hungarian lady made. And it was good. So they interchanged. You've got to know that this is like a melting pot. My Aunt Anna Markovich, who was Slovak, worked in an elegant hotel in Austria before she came to this country and learned to make butter pastries which now our entire family makes, so now we call them Slovak Kolacky.

Food is, nevertheless, a vital symbol of ethnicity, and its preparation and consumption offer significant opportunities to create, reinforce, and revise group ties while enacting a sense of ethnic identity. Baking and cooking are significant to the development and maintenance of ethnic identity and community primarily because they are embedded in other group activities and relationships within groups. Charlotte Filka described how participating in Holy Rosary baking days was inextricably part of family life and parish life for her and her siblings:

This is the fourth generation for our family. My mother went to this school and her mother was one of the first parishioners here. That was my Grandma Kocan. And then my mother came to the school; her name was Helen Kocan. Then we came to this school, my mother's four kids. Then after her four kids, our kids all went here. Now our grandchildren are here. Isn't that amazing? It is not basically just all about baking. We just love to be together. It is a parish. We as a family—there are two brothers and two sisters—we all belong. And we all work. And we all work this baking, and festivals—you name it, we do it.

Such family connections within baking groups were not unusual; learning to bake and practicing took place within a larger complex of relationships and activities.

While one needs to be part of a group to bake successfully, one can also become part of a group through participation in activities such as baking. Ann Mascsak explained how her non-Hungarian sister-in-law became "Hungarian:"

We call her our 'Hungarian Hillbilly.' She was married to my brother [who is now deceased]. *My mother taught her how to make these Hungarian cookies and hers are much better than mine. She has just got the lightest touch. My mother always told us the less you handle the dough, the flakier it is going to be, so don't take your rolling pin and press on it. Just very lightly. Well, Lorraine, you know, her cookies are just out of this world. She only lived about three doors from where my mother lived. So my mother was there quite a bit and then Lorraine would be at my mom's house, so she would show her how to cook all these Hungarian foods. And she did real well. She learned everything.*

Thus "being ethnic" is less a matter of one's inheriting by direct descent, or "owning" a certain, comprehensive group of skills and knowledge, than it is a matter of communicating and interacting with a group of people with whom one identifies based on a sense of shared history and traditions. Just as learning to bake depends on one's working over time with expert bakers as well as reading a recipe, being (or becoming) a member of an ethnic group depends on one's interacting over time with a community as well as knowing particular traditions.

* * * * *

The author thanks the people who shared their

knowledge, experience, and recipes: Judy Balogh, Joyce Baker, Jean Biro, Virginia Chorba, Margaret Feudi, Charlotte Filka, Katherine Galatocky, Margaret Hayden, Marge Juhafc, Lillian Keil, Anna Keller, Jerri Kucera, Pat Markos, Ann Mascsak, Agnes Gadus McDaniel, Grace Molnar, Virginia Molnar, Judy Paulsen, Susan Haydu Pohlman, Helen Powers, Catherine Soltis, Irene Stuller, Anna Swanson, Anne Walko, Anna May Zajcz, and John Zajcz.

Quoted material is transcribed from audiotape with the exception of ellipses . . . indicating that a word or passage was omitted, and brackets [ ] indicating that words were added to clarify meaning. Transcripts are available in the University of Toledo Folklore Archives. Lists of other potential interviewees not used here are included in the UT Folklore Archives as well.

The Ritual of Sutni Saluna

by Andrew Ludanyi

The Szollozi men enjoy a backyard sutni

Those Birmingham customs tied to festive occasions such as Christmas and Easter tended to survive intact. These were church-related affairs and thus received official institutional backing. But those customs tied to everyday life were harder to maintain. When workers came home from their days at the National Malleable Castings Corporation factory, they were exhausted.

Real blood, sweat, and tears were involved and they didn't leave much time for practicing folk customs for their own sake. Some grandmothers continued to embroider and some individuals consciously nurtured their Hungarian folk culture. But the average person did not have the time to do so. But there were customs that could be practiced on weekends and during breaks in the working week. One prime example is the sutni, a session of grilling bacon over an open fire.

Sutni [pronounced shoot-ny] is the infinitive form of the word sutes, which means roasting. The correct Hungarian name is szalonna sutes, but people in Birmingham have generally used the abbreviated form. Sutni does not require special attention or a great deal of time. It is also functional. When you have a sutni, you feed yourself, which you have to do regardless of overwork and exhaustion. Sutni is a meal and a social occasion, a chance to sit, talk, and visit.

Although it originated as a folk custom, by the turn of the century sutni was mostly practiced by middle-class Hungarians. When they went picnicking, they did a sutni.

Peasants, the farming and working classes, had szalonnazas where they sat down at a table, took a knife and cut the bacon, then ate it with a fork or put it on bread for a sandwich.

Around 1900, sutni as a social custom became very popular with those who wanted to get away from the urban areas on weekends and holidays. When they did leave the cities, Hungarians went to parks where they would build a fire and cut a stick to carve into a spit or nyars. Chunks of bacon were skewered onto the sharpened end of the nyars. The chunks were sliced in patterns with a knife (and there are many opinions about how this is supposed to be done), then the nyars was placed over the fire.

The sutni was, and is, a group effort. Ten or fifteen people gather around the fire, each with his own nyars. The drippings from the bacon are combined with onions, good bread, and sometimes strong green peppers. Interestingly, tomatoes were never part of old-country sutni. The BLT, bacon, lettuce and tomato sandwich, is an American invention and that may be the reason for the addition of tomato to the Birmingham recipe. Every person can make his own version and combination.

Some important additions to the ritual have also been developed. Everyone needs something to help the bacon slide down the nyars. Beer, good wine, or palinka [strong fruit brandy] are as important in northeastern Hungary as in Birmingham. And nowadays, a twirler—the host or someone who is responsible for the sutni—is essential. This person cuts up bread, tomatoes, onions, and peppers ahead of time and usually is the first to begin to"twirl" the bacon over the wood fire.

The twirler who hosts the sutni is usually an older person because it's important to have an expert who knows how not to burn the bacon which makes it bitter. There's a fine line between burning and undercooking; the twirler is one with lots of experience in this art. One interesting innovation I've seen at the Birmingham Festival is a machine that does the twirling and making the nyars.

The wood also has to be special. While this is a point of considerable debate, the Birmingham consensus is that fruit tree wood, especially cherry, is best. Pine can't be used because it smokes too much.

What role do the women play in the sutni ritual? Basically, none. It is the man's domain, like American charcoal grilling. The host is usually male, and most of the participants close to the fire are men. I have never seen a woman do the sutni in Birmingham.

The sutni's physical setting has also changed over the years. Instead of a number of small fires on the ground, the sutni has evolved to fit in a middle-class backyard, with the participants taking turns using one fire, similar to the American backyard grill. The twirler now sets things up like an assembly line or conveyor belt. The bread is neatly stacked, each piece getting its share of drippings in turn. It is a very efficient—and very American—system.

The social atmosphere of the sutni has not been lost, however. Having a good time with family and friends still remains. And the sutni is almost always multi-generational. A typical gathering will include grandparents, parents, and children of several families. The sutni saluna reinforces Hungarian-ness without drawing self-conscious attention to it and without requiring a great deal of specialized preparation or training.

The Betlehemes játék Christmas Play

by Raymond J. Pentzell

The St. Stephen's Abauj Betlehemes troop at Monoky's Cafe. The Öregs, with their axes, are in front. The Betlehemes creche is in the center.

Few Toledoans are aware that an ancient Hungarian folk play is performed every Christmas season in the streets and houses of the Birmingham neighborhood on the city's East Side. After living and teaching in Toledo for a number of years, I learned of its existence from a student in a theatre history class who appeared singularly unimpressed by the mysteriousness of the British folk plays I was discussing.

"Oh, we have all that over on the East Side every year," he told me. "In Birmingham, the Hungarians do it. It's a Bethlehem Shepherds play, but it's got all that boogie-man stuff in it too." Thus I encountered the Betlehemes játék, a folk Christmas play familiar in every part of Hungary and in the Hungarian communities of Romania, Slovakia, and the former Yugoslavia.

Local Birmingham tradition says that the Bethlehem play has been presented yearly since the arrival of the Hungarians in the 1890s, and under informal parish sponsorship from the time St. Stephen's Catholic Church was founded in 1898. The scripts, as well as performance elements, provide virtually indisputable internal evidence of an unbroken oral tradition reaching directly back to Hungary.

Birmingham residents call the play the Abauj Bethlehem play, but no records or traditions survive that point to any specific town of origin. Photographs of Toledo performances survive from the early twentieth century. The Bethlehem play is no synthetic "folkloristic" revival staged by sentimental Hungarophiles. Residents can recall only a few odd years (for example, once during World War II) when none of the three available troupes "came out."

Two troupes, called the Elsö and Második ("first" and "second"), are formed from St. Stephen's congregation. Each is organized by ties of family and friendship. The lines of succession to the roles are guarded by the transmission of performance coaching and the inheritance of costumes.

Continuity is taken most seriously by the troupe leaders, who normally succeed to the coveted role of principal Öreg, the demonic "old man." The third troupe was made up of parishioners of St. Michael's Byzantine Catholic Church, formerly just three blocks from St. Stephen's. They claimed a tradition of performance from the founding of the parish in 1914, but actual memories or records of a St. Michael's troupe extend no further back than the 1930s.

The community's rationale for maintaining the custom was, in part, the collection of Christmas donations to the Church, since each performance ended in a quête. But it is important to note that laymen alone assigned and played the roles, that the troupe leader was also a player, and that costumes, properties, and whatever memoranda pass for scripts were made and kept by each player's own family. Scripts, however, were mimeographed in full by St. Michael's troupe, though not St. Stephen's. A parish's clergy officially did no more than "encourage" the performance or, in some years, merely permitted it.

In the early and mid-1970s, the Birmingham community underwent a renewal of pride in its identity and traditions which grew out of the successful collective political action first mobilized to oppose plans for building an expressway overpass through the neighborhood.

One by-product was a resurgence of participation in the nearly moribund Bethlehem plays among the adults of St. Stephen's. In 1973, interest was so low that St. Stephen's did not send out a troupe. In 1974, St. Stephen's mounted a full-strength adult troupe (Második) of fluent Hungarian speakers. In 1976, the Elsö troupe, dormant since 1970, was revived. Aided by a grant from the National Endowment for the Arts, a documentary film was made in 1976, produced by Peter Ujvagi.

A Betlehem troupe at full strength consists of eight young men: three shepherds, two angels, and about three öregek,"old ones."In both of the St. Stephen's versions, three shepherds and one öreg have speaking roles; only two of the shepherds had lines, in St. Michael's version. Even in a skeleton cast, however, there will be two angels who carry the Betlehem and sing and more than one öreg. Residents remember performances with as many as a half dozen öregek, since the character is popular and fun to play.

The costumes of the shepherds and angels are almost identical—flowing white blouses with loose, uncuffed sleeves resembling an acolyte's surplice and full, ankle-length white skirts, sometimes trimmed at bottom with lace or fringe. An older tradition, still maintained by some players, substitutes white gátyák (the broad, skirtlike culottes once worn by Magyar plainsmen) for the skirts.

St. Stephen's players have wide shoulder sashes crossed on their chests and backs, waist sashes, and bows at their necks where the wide ribbons that secure the hats are tied. Old photographs show various ways of distinguishing angels and shepherds by sash color. In recent times the Elsö troupe is distinguished only by hat color, as all sashes are red. The Második troupe keeps the angels in red; the First Shepherd's sashes are white with red edging; the Second has a red waist-sash and green shoulder-sashes; the Third has a green waist-sash and red shoulder-sashes.

At St. Michael's, the angels' crossed shoulder sashes were pink (right shoulder) and pale blue (left), while those of the shepherds were red (right shoulder) and green (left). Neither bows nor waistbands were worn (they are absent as well in one older photograph of a St. Stephen's troupe).

All troupes wore tall, brimless hats of shiny cardboard, about sixteen inches high, painted or appliquéd with paper and foil and hung with ribbons fastened at the top. At St. Stephen's the hats are in the shape of truncated cones, colored in various combinations of white, red, green, blue, and gold, with large crosses, stars, and rosettes emblazoned on the front.

Two old photographs (1913 and c.1914) show the hats to be fully conical, about two feet tall. The St. Michael's players' hats were more nearly cylindrical, painted in broad horizontal bands of Hungary's colors—red, white, and green; near the top, on the red band, a small Byzantine cross is painted in gold. Shepherds of both churches carried straight poles, about five feet long and an inch and a half in diameter, with "jinglers" (as on a tambourine) nailed to the top. At St. Michael's the poles were painted in foot-wide bands of red, white, and green; at St. Stephen's red and white are customary.

The two angels carry between them the Betlehem, a model church with a wide portal, inside which are the figures of the crêche. Money collected at performances is sometimes kept in the Betlehem; in fact, the 1973 St. Michael's Betlehem held no figurines, only a cigar box. An old (pre-1920) photograph of a St. Stephen's troupe shows the two angels holding cavalry sabers. No one I spoke to remembered any hint of this practice.

The "white-clad" shepherd costume, common but not universal in Hungary for these roles, is derived from that of the angels, in direct descent from frequent practice in medieval liturgical drama.

Öreg means "old one" or "old man." It is used in a strictly denotative context and also familiarly. A different form of the Hungarian word for old, regös, is the categorical name of Christmas waits, variously costumed carolers and pranksters (originally shamanic) not appearing in plays. The öregek of the Toledo Betlehem plays are recognizably demonic, particular variants of the wild-man or fur-demon mummers known throughout Europe, although in the play script the Old Man's lines suggest that he is no more than a deaf, cranky, lazy, blasphemous old shepherd.

The players I spoke to explained the apparent paradox in a variety of ways.

"He is supposed to be a pagan who worships the devil and acts like one."

"He is really the devil, the old one, come to tempt the other shepherds."

"The word öreg—old man—sounds something like ördög—devil. And he's just a rotten old funny bastard."

Öreg players improvise their own costumes with some exuberance, but always within certain bounds. An öreg in Toledo will always wear a full bag-mask made of fur and a fur vest or jacket; he will always brandish a real (but blunted) ax, painted red and white, and have a pouch or satchel slung over his shoulder; one or more cowbells will be tied to his belt or his legs.

Certain other traditions are not so binding: white duck trousers (or baseball knickers) stuffed into canvas army leggings or high boots, a red sweater or sweatshirt under the fur jacket, a small cross embroidered somewhere on the fur (or painted on the cowbells). Some öregek wear sheepskin jackets (or jacket liners) turned fur-side-out;

most construct or inherit shaggy jackets cut from old fur coats, to which are sewn tails, old mink collars, and ragged strips of any kind of pelt.

Bag-masks show considerable variety, with yarn embroidery around mouth, nose, and eyeholes, and pieces of cheap wigs or contrasting fur sewn on as mustaches, beards, or general decoration. Many öregek sport horns or long ears—turkey feathers rising out of knots of fur, fox or raccoon tails. Sometimes the bag-mask itself is shaped rather like an inverted trapezoid; stuffing pushed into the two upper corners is enough to provide bulbous "ears."

Since World War II, the angels have usually been thirteen to sixteen years old, and the shepherds and öregek young men between seventeen and twenty-five. After 1974, both St. Stephen's troupes were reconstituted with players emerging from "retirement." The Elsö players, led by Joseph Karocki, were then mostly in their late 20s or early 30s; the more polished Második troupe, then led by Stephen Pompos, were made up primarily of men in their 40s.

Since then, of course, the roles have passed on to a newer generation. Many older local men remember continuing their roles into their thirties and pre-war photographs bear this out. It used to be assumed that a performer would quit when he got married, although there was never a strict rule governing this; married men simply were assumed to have less free time during the Christmas holidays.

The players' ages may be important to the question of the traditionalism of the Toledo versions of the play. In present-day Hungary, many variants, chiefly those in cities, larger towns, and suburban villages, are done entirely by children and adolescents, and in some places—for example, Mezökövesd, Borsod County—by girls. Young adult-male troupes, evidently the older tradition, have been retained primarily in the more remote rural areas, notably among the Székely people of the Transylvania mountains.

In both Toledo churches, the players form a procession at the beginning of the Christmas Midnight Mass. Shepherds and angels proceed up the center aisle in full costume, hats on, the angels carrying the Betlehem. The öregek, however, do not wear their fur masks and generally keep some steps to the rear.

All sing folk carols, first at the back of the church and then during their slow march: "Mondjátok Mag Jó Pásztorok, Miket Láttakok?" ("Tell us, good shepherds, what have you seen?"); "Szent, Szent, Szent Vagy, Nagy Ur Isten" ("Holy, holy, holy are you, great Lord God"); "Istengyermek, kit irgalmad közénk lehozott" ("God's Child, who through suffering has been brought to us"); "O gyönyörü szép, titokzatos éj" ("O wondrously beautiful night of mystery"); and "Ha kimegyek ajtom elé" ("If I step outside the door"). At St. Michael's, the procession was usually followed by a performance of the play before the altar, but this had not been the case at St. Stephen's until 1976, when such performances became customary.

No particular spiritual benefit is thought to derive from participation other than the virtue of earning money for the Church. Players and former players are unanimous in denying even the vaguest superstition of good luck in performing the play, unlike many mummers in England and elsewhere. As in most American Christmas customs, the chief objectives are the fun of celebration and the maintenance of a group-identifying tradition.

Traditionally, at least through the 1970s, the scenario was as follows: In late morning or early afternoon of Christmas Eve and Christmas Day the players take to the streets. They know roughly which houses they will perform in, on the basis of past welcomes, awareness that family parties will be going on, or simply by mutual agreement. Some householders, but not all, have given them explicit invitations, and they in turn may have given the residents an idea when to expect them. Scheduling is expected for performances at the corner taverns, sites of great applause and generous donations on Christmas Eve.

On the street, the shepherds and angels walk in a group, with some dignity, though not solemnity. Occasionally they sing the carols used in the church procession. As the shepherds mark their steps with their poles, the jingling becomes rhythmic. The öregek meanwhile, race up and down the blocks yelling and waving their axes, with their cowbells clanking, in uproarious attempts to frighten children and kiss girls.

It was customary through the 1950s for the öregek to pilfer groceries from the shops; all food was dutifully donated to the convent, though wine always mysteriously vanished by day's end. The neighborhood children pelt them with snowballs (the angels' and shepherds' hats are also fine targets), and occasionally more dangerous projectiles, so that it sometimes takes a particularly cool-headed öreg to avoid a brawl.

In 1972, an öreg was detained by the police, and a parish priest spent some time overcoming non-Magyar skepticism before the öreg was given back his "dangerous weapon" and let out of the police car with a warning. In 1975, a St. Michael's öreg was struck with his own ax, luckily without permanent injury.

At the door of a house or bar, one of the shepherds or angels announces their presence. There is no separate runner or envoy as in many versions in Hungary. Shouted welcomes greet them. The angels enter and place the Betlehem on a table or chair. The shepherds follow, beating the jingling poles rhythmically on the floor. The öregek remain on the porch peering in the windows and doorway while cracking jokes, or in bad weather, they slink or leap into the room and roam around the edges of the gathering, growling, kissing girls, and jocularly insulting audience members. The shepherds and angels arrange themselves in a rough semicircle in the center of the space and, to the tapping of the poles, sing a song which the öregek may join in singing if they feel like it. The play proper has begun.

Each of the troupes has a different version of the play, though all are similar. St. Stephen's players learn their lines by rote from fathers and older brothers, and while written speeches are used to aid learning, they are saved, if at all, only by the players' families. A troupe leader knows the whole play by heart, as do the more experienced players, and at the few preliminary run-throughs, newcomers are helped over lapses of memory.

At St. Michael's, however, while rehearsal procedures were similar, there were written texts, one in Hungarian and one in English, which had been repeatedly mimeographed and distributed. Copies were kept both at the church and by individual families.

No one now remembers who first set down the St. Michael's play in writing, but informants agree that the script has not changed since the 1930s. It is not clear how much liberty the St. Michael's players felt they could take with their speeches. In the mimeographed script, dotted lines indicated places where the Öreg is free to add comic lines.

The St. Michael's troupe I accompanied in 1973 kept to the Hungarian script verbatim, but they were quick to point out that no one among them was fluent enough in Hungarian to trust himself at improvising. For the required ad-lib points, the Öreg had memorized condensed versions of speeches from one of the St. Stephen's versions.

The St. Michael's players were prepared to act the play in either Hungarian or English at the audience's request. The mimeographed English version, in a more pompous and awkward style than the Hungarian, was not a close translation. When the 1973 troupe played in English, they virtually ignored it, opting instead for a combination of direct translation and wild ad-libbing. In English, both the written script and the performers' version substituted carols familiar in America (O Come All Ye Faithful, The First Noel, Silent Night) for the Hungarian songs.

Ad-libbing is not the best term for some of their digressions, for a number of unwritten lines are themselves considered traditional. Of note is the name Pedro, by which the Öreg was addressed in performance; it does not appear in either the St. Michael's or the St. Stephen's Hungarian versions, or in the "official" English script of St. Michael's.

When asked, "Why Pedro?" the players' answer was

simply, "That's his name. It's what he's always called when we act in English." It is possible that the name results from a inside joke, the point of which is now forgotten. It is at least equally probable that Pedro's origin lies in genuine Hungarian tradition. In scattered towns in the North-Central region from which Toledo's Hungarians first emigrated, the counterpart of the Öreg is called Kecskés Peti (Goatherd Pete), the proper name itself possibly a borrowing from Slovak tradition.

In Toledo, Peti may have been contaminated with the Hungarian word pedrö ("twisting, turning"), although this is a mere conjecture. The name Peter for a wild-man or Christmas Percht is common: Pedro Serrano, Peter the Wild Boy of Hannover, Black Peter (Spanish-costumed) who accompanies St. Nicholas into Amsterdam, among others.

Neither of St. Stephen's troupes performs in English. The plays are somewhat more informal than the St. Michael's script, full of nonsequiturs, slang, and dialect. By the same token, St. Stephen's players less often feel the urge to improvise; their respect for the plays' presumed authenticity works against this. The St. Stephen's Második script is the longest and seems to contain the greatest number of parallels with older, native Hungarian Betlehem plays.

This is not to say that it is more authentic than the other two; all show ample evidence of faithful descent—each, probably, from a different Hungarian village. St. Stephen's Elsö and the St. Michael's variants have essentially the same plot as the Második play, but both omit a most interesting sequence: the sudden "falling asleep" of the Öreg soon after his entrance.

Except where noted, Alex Helm and E. C. Cawte's remark about the older British mummers' plays holds for the Toledo Hungarian performances: "For the most part they stood in a semi-circle: as needed, each stepped forward, uttered his lines in a loud voice with no inflections, and stepped back."

This is not done with mechanical rigidity, however,

and lines are spoken, not intoned. There is no goal of "ritualizing" the speech, as the better actors, those more comfortable in Hungarian, speak with as much expression as they can muster within the limits of an artificial loudness and stilted physical movement.

The translation that follows is based on the text used since 1974 by Stephen Pompos' troupe and its successors, the same script that those returning players learned and played in the 1950s. It was transcribed and translated literally for me by Peter Ujvagi.

The Betlehemes játék Play: St. Stephen's Second Troupe

translated by Peter Ujvagi

The Betlehem creche

ENTRANCE SONG: Everywhere may joy be heard. The Messiah, all behold, has been born the Son of God, as the Scriptures have foretold. The redeemer of mankind, who from death will us unbind, in the cold is shivering. Alle-Alleluia!

FIRST SHEPHERD: (Bows to Betlehem) Praise to Jesus! (To audience) I beg your pardon for coming into your house without a word. Even a shepherd will take himself to the kind of place where he's out of the cold and can feel himself in a nice, warm room. I was afraid to stay alone out in the woods. I have seen some kind of scary spook. I thought something's going to come of this and nobody can knock it out of my head. (To Second Shepherd) Come in, my friend.

SECOND SHEPHERD: (Bows to Betlehem) Praise to Jesus! (To First Shepherd) Lucky I found you here. You're just the one I've been looking for, because I admit I was scared to be alone. All my life I've been a shepherd, nothing else, and I don't run away, not even from my own shadow! But the sheep and lambs are bleating in fear! (To Householder) Ai! My master's son, maybe they're chasing me! So then I picked myself up and started running for real, to get with my close friends. Maybe I've left them behind for good.

THIRD SHEPHERD: (Bows to Betlehem) Praise to Jesus! (To Second Shepherd) Friend, how come you've pitched yourself all the way here, when you know very well you should never leave the flock?

SECOND SHEPHERD: I wouldn't have left them, except a spook chased me and scared me so much . . . whoo! I still shake thinking about it!

THIRD SHEPHERD: (Waving staff) Where is this spook? Let me give it such a whack that its clothes will burst apart! (To Second Shepherd) You ought to be driving a wagon, not tending our flock! Just let any old spook stand here in front of me!

OREG: (Bounding into center of room; other öregek start growling at audience from the side) A sausagey good evening to you, my dear little children. (To audience generally) Well! Do you all just sit here eating and drinking and sucking tobacco smoke and never giving a thought to your old Dad? Sure, if I take out this old ax, I'll crack you in the neck so hard even I'll regret it! I'm going to plop down this rotten old smelly sinful body right in the midst of you. (He begins to lie down and sprawl on his back.) Oh, my friends, what have I really won? Here I've lost my old sheepskin coat and my staff, and for what? (In disgust) Just so I could come to see little Jesus! (He drops off to sleep.)

FIRST SHEPHERD: Listen, my shepherd companions. No other song is like this one.

ALL: Lift your head high. With your ears listen well.

ANGELS: This child has stamped at the gates of Hell!

FIRST SHEPHERD: Old Man!

ALL: He has forced open the gates of Hell, the gates of Hell!

FIRST SHEPHERD: Up, my friends, arise. Be quick, the hour flies! The angels bring us warning the Messiah is aborning! Let's up and go! Move out, you, ho!

ALL: Let's up and go, the miracle to see. To God's Son let us go on bended knee. Of Mary He is born, for us this Christmas morn, In Bethlehem, in Bethlehem.

FIRST ANGEL: (Spoken) Gloria.

FIRST SHEPHERD: (To sleeping Öreg) Listen, Old Man! Do you hear?

ÖREG: (From floor, waving ax at First Shepherd) May your eyeballs run out of their sockets!

SECOND ANGEL: (Spoken) Gloria in excelsis Deo.

FIRST SHEPHERD: Listen, Old Man! The sheep have run into the corncrib! Three hundred and thirty-six thistle-burrs are stuck in their tails! When are you going to get them out?

ÖREG: (Still on floor, moans his line as if not yet awake) Oh, by tomorrow or else tonight sometime. (Shepherds jingle their poles.)

FIRST SHEPHERD: Let's chop some wood under the Old Man. (Shepherds prod Öreg with their poles.)

ÖREG: Under your Granny's knee! (Gets up.) Oh, how sweetly was I sleeping, and I dreamt three beautiful girls came to tell me that tonight the Messiah was born, who will save the whole world. They said, "Let's go and adore Jesus in Bethlehem!"

FIRST SHEPHERD: Old Man, will you cross yourself? (Gestures a Sign of the Cross hurriedly.)

ÖREG: You want me to toss myself? What, turn cartwheels? [In Hungarian, close puns.]

FIRST SHEPHERD: No, Old Man, that's not how it's done.

We'll make the Sign of the Cross, Old Man.

ÖREG: And how do you do that?

FIRST SHEPHERD: (Demonstrating the gestures carefully) To the Father . . . and the Son . . .

ÖREG: (Parodying him with clownish mockery) Chicken meat . . .goose meat . . . one, two, down my gullet it slides. [In Hungarian, more puns.]

FIRST SHEPHERD: Not that way, Old Man!

ÖREG: Well then, how?

FIRST SHEPHERD: In the name of the Father, and of the Son, and of the Holy Ghost, Amen.

ÖREG: You better not say it that way in front of me, you big jackass! (Öreg makes the sign of the cross.)

FIRST SHEPHERD: Now you ought to pray, Old Man!

ÖREG: (In a mincing recitation) Our Father, if thou art, I'll go along. But lead us not into Munkacs [A real city and a pun on the Hungarian word for "work."] but deliver us to Debrecen instead, for some good wheat bread.

FIRST SHEPHERD: Sing, Old Man! (All the öregek dance

in the center of the room, a jogging reel to the beating of the shepherds' poles on the floor.)

ÖREGEK: (Singing in scratchy voices) The old hick had it easy up to now. He never would get married anyhow. But now that he's over the hill, he hasn't a cent in the till—that worn-out old yokel.

FIRST SHEPHERD: That's no song, Old Man!

ÖREG: What is it then?

FIRST SHEPHERD: Curses! Swearwords! Filth!

ÖREG: Then you all sing something better and prettier! (Threateningly) But you better not laugh!

SHEPHERDS: Come to Bethlehem, my friends, my friends.

ANGELS: There we'll have a perfect home, a home. We'll never have to hoe the vines, the vines. But even so we'll drink the wine, the wine. Stroll, you flutist. Pipe a tune, a tune. Back and forth and halt your stride. Back and forth and halt your stride. Shake, Old Man, your old fur hide, fur hide, and give your fleas a dizzy ride, a ride.

FIRST SHEPHERD: (Goes to the Betlehem creche and genuflects) My dear little Jesus, I've come to you and brought you gold, frankincense, and myrrh. [No real props are used here.]

SECOND SHEPHERD: (Same business) My dear little Jesus, I've come to you too. I've brought you a little lamb.

THIRD SHEPHERD: (Same business) My dear little Jesus, I've come to you too. I've brought you a little piece of cheese.

FIRST SHEPHERD: (To Öreg) Come with us, Old Man, to Bethlehem.

ÖREG: (Bumbling around room) Where to? Where to? To Debrecen? To make a little pipe? [*Kis pipat csinalni*—to make a little pipe—is thought by the players to be merely the Öreg's nonsense.]

FIRST SHEPHERD: No, Old Man! No, let us go to Bethlehem and adore little Jesus.

ÖREG: (Peering into the Betlehem creche) But which one is little Jesus? The one with the big horns?

FIRST SHEPHERD: Ox, Old Man! Ox!

ÖREG: Well then, which one? The one with the long ears?

But that one's behind my back! (Reference to both the creche donkey and the First Shepherd.)

FIRST SHEPHERD: Donkey, Old Man! Donkey! No, Old Man. He's lying in the manger.

ÖREG: (Kneeling, bows deeply or else sprawls headlong on the floor in front of the Betlehem) Now I see you, my little Jesus! I've come to you too, dragging a cow and a sack of bread on my back. (Sometimes he names a local bakery.) I know how little children love milk! (Stands) But I'd rather drink it myself. I won't give it to you.

FIRST SHEPHERD: Quiet, Old Man! I see you trying to haggle over milk and bread!

ÖREG: I give it freely.

ALL SING: May God keep this householder's house from all harm. May God fill his cellars and silos and barn. We thank you, good host; let us be on our way. But on all of your household may God's blessing stay. [During this last song the players collect money that is stashed away in the Betlehem or in the satchels of the öregek.]

Selected Readings

Introduction —

Ahern, John F., Ed. *Birmingham Remembers: Transcriptions of Video-taped Interviews 1983-84, Volume I, Toledo, Ohio.* Joint project of the Department of History and the Urban Affairs Center at the University of Toledo and the Toledo-Lucas County Public Library, 1984.

The Preservation of Ethnic Heritage: An Examination of the Birmingham Experience. Toledo. The University of Toledo College of Education and Allied Professions, 1987.

Roots in Birmingham. Toledo, Ohio. Joint project of the Department of History and the Urban Affairs Center at the University of Toledo and the Toledo-Lucas County Public Library, 1997.

Bartha, Stephen J. *A History of Immigrant Groups in Toledo: A Thesis.* Columbus, Ohio: Ohio State University, 1945.

Britton, Diane F. and John F. Ahern, Eds. *Birmingham:*

Reflections on Community. Toledo, Ohio. Joint Project of the Department of History and the Urban Affairs Center at the University of Toledo and the Toledo-Lucas County Public Library, 1992.

Czigany, Lorant, Ed. *Hungarica: Catalogue of the Bela Ivanyi-Grunwald Collection.* London: Szepsi Csombor Literary Circle, 1967.

Domotor, Tekla. *Hungarian Folk Beliefs.* Bloomington: Indiana University Press, 1981.

Fel, Edit and Thomas Hofer. *Proper Peasants: Traditional Life in a Hungarian Village.* Chicago: Aldine Press, 1969.

Hann, C.M. *Tazlar: A Village in Hungary.* Cambridge and New York: Cambridge University Press, 1980.

Hrivnyak, John M. *Birmingham: Toledo's Hungarian Community.* Master's thesis, University of Toledo, 1975.

Konnyu, Leslie. *A Condensed Geography of Hungary.* St. Louis: The American Hungarian Review, 1971.

Lengyl, Emil. *Americans from Hungary.* Philadelphia: J. B. Lippincott, 1948.

The Land and People of Hungary. Philadelphia: J.B. Lippincott, 1972.

Michaels, Larry R. *East Side Story: Peoples and Places in the History of East Toledo.* Toledo: Bihl House Publishing, 1993.

Puskas, Julianna. *From Hungary to the United States, 1880-1940.* Budapest: Academiai Kiado, 1982.

Sarfalvi, Bela, ed. *The Changing Face of the Great Hungarian Plain.* Budapest: Akademiai Kiado, 1971.

Sinor, Denis. *History of Hungary.* Westport, Connecticut: Greenwood Press Publishers, 1976.

Sozan, Michael. *The History of Hungarian Ethnography.* Washington, D.C.: University Press of America, 1977.

Szeplaki, Joseph, Ed. *Doctoral Dissertations Related to Hungary Accepted in the United States and Canada, and Bibliographies on Hungary.* Athens, Ohio: Ohio University Library, 1974.

Szuch, Yolanda Danyi. *The History of St. Stephen's Church.* Toledo, Ohio: privately printed, 1993.

Vardy, Stephen Bela. *The Hungarian-Americans.* Boston:

Twayne Publishers, 1985.

Wright, Isaac. *The East Side Past and Present.* Toledo: Second Congregational Church of Toledo, 1894.

Zieren, Gregory Robert. *The Propertied Worker: Working Class Formation in Toledo, Ohio 1870-1900.* Dissertation, University of Delaware, 1981.

Church and Community

"A Church's Response to the Preservation of Ethnic Heritage: Religious Traditions at St. Stephen's Church," in *The Preservation of Ethnic Heritage: An Examination of the Birmingham Experience. Toledo.* The University of Toledo College of Education and Allied Professions, 1987.

Beecher, Lucas J. "The Magyars in Toledo." *Toledo Blade,* January 26, 1907.

Bell, Daniel. "Ethnicity and Social Change" in *Ethnicity: Theory and Practice.* Nathan Glazer and Daniel P. Moynihan, eds. Cambridge: Harvard University Press, 1975.

Britton, Diane F. and John F. Ahern, Eds. *Birmingham:*

Reflections on Community. Toledo, Ohio. Joint project of the Department of History and the Urban Affairs Center at the University of Toledo and the Toledo-Lucas County Public Library, 1992.

Daniels, Roger. *Coming to America.* New York: Harper Perennial, 1990.

Domotor, Tekla. *Hungarian Folk Beliefs.* Bloomington: Indiana University Press, 1981.

Fishman, Joshua A. *Hungarian Language Maintenance in the United States.* Bloomington: Indiana University Press, 1966.

Hrivnyak, John M. "Birmingham: Toledo's Hungarian Community." Master's thesis, University of Toledo, 1975.

Jasco, Paul. "The Jasco Family." 1984. Birmingham Cultural Center, Toledo, Ohio.

Jubilate—1899-1924: St. Stephen's Parish Jubilee. Toledo: American-Hungarian Printing Co., 1924.

Lengyl, Emil. *Americans from Hungary.* Philadelphia: J.B. Lippincott Company, 1948.

Ludanyi, Julianna Nadas. "Hungarian Wedding Customs." 1992. Toledo-Lucas County Public Library, Birmingham branch.

Miller, Randall M. and Thomas D. Marzik, eds. *Immigration and Religion in Urban America.* Philadelphia: Temple University Press, 1977.

Pecseyne, Steve. 1984. Department of Archives and Manuscripts, Toledo-Lucas County Public Library.

Puskas, Julianna. *From Hungary to the United States 1880-1914.* Budapest: Akademiai Kiado, 1982.

Swiderski, Richard M. *Teaching Language, Learning Culture.* Westport, Conneticut: Bergin and Garrey, 1993.

Szuch, Yolanda Danya. "The History of St. Stephen's Church." Toledo, Ohio: privately printed, 1993.

Toledo, Ohio. Joint Project of the Department of History and the Urban Affairs Center at the University of Toledo and the Toledo-Lucas County Public Library, 1984.

Urban Turf and Ethnic Soul: An American Neighborhood's Struggle for Survival. Videotape. Toledo and Ada,

Ohio, the Birmingham community and Ohio Northern University. 1985.

Vardy, Stephan Bela. *The Hungarian-Americans.* Boston: Twayne Publishers, 1985.

Vasko, Jerry. "Recollections About Abauj Betlehemes." In *The Preservation of Ethnic Heritage,* 1987.

Walch, Timothy. *Catholicism in America.* Florida: Robert E. Krieger Publishing Company, 1989.

Zieren, Gregory Robert. "The Propertied Worker: Working Class Formation in Toledo, Ohio 1870-1900." Dissertation. University of Delaware, 1981.

Birmingham Folk Narratives —

Aarne, Antti and Stith Thompson. *The Types of the Folktale: A Classification and Bibliography, Second Revision.* Helsinki: Academia Scientarum Fennica, 1961.

Baughman, Richard. "Differential Identity and the Social Base of Folklore." *Journal of American Folklore 84* (1971), pp. 31-41.

Barth, Frederick. *Ethnic Groups and Boundaries.* New York: Cambridge University Press, 1969.

Dégh, Linda. "Survival and Revival of European Folk Cultures in America." In Ethnologia Europaea 2-3 (1968-1969). *Of Cultural Pluralism: An Evaluative Sourcebook.* Aurora, Ill., 1974.

Kirshenblatt-Gimblett, Barbara. "Traditional Storytelling in the Toronto Jewish Community: A Study in Performance and Creativity in an Immigrant Culture." Dissertation. Indiana University, 1972.

Kolm, Richard. *Bibliography of Ethnicity and Ethnic Groups.* Rockville, Maryland, 1973.

Krappe, Alexander Haggerty. "American' Folklore." In *Folk-Say: A Regional Miscellany,* Benjamin Botkin, ed. Norman, Oklahoma, 1930. pp. 291-97.

Martin, Wallace. *Recent Theories of Narrative.* Ithaca: Cornell University Press, 1986.

Stern, Stephen. "Ethnic Folklore and the Folklore of Ethnicity." In *Western Folklore 36,* (1977), No. 1.

Birmingham Architecture —

Beecher, Lucas J. "Magyars: Children of Nature Who Have Abandoned The Broad Hungarian Prairies for Giant Iron Mills of the East Side." *Toledo Blade*, January 26, 1907.

Divald, Kornel. *Old Hungarian Art.* Oxford University Press, 1931.

Fel, Edit and Tamas Hofer. *Proper Peasants: Traditional Life in a Hungarian Village.* Chicago: Aldine Publishing Co., 1969.

Gambos, Zoltan, ed. *Hungarians in America.* Cleveland: Szabadsag, 1941.

Gero, Laszlo. *Hungarian Architecture Until the End of the Nineteenth Century.* Budapest: Epitesugyi Kiado, 1954.

Hempel, Eberhard. *Baroque Art and Architecture in Central Europe.* Baltimore: Penguin Books, 1965.

Hrivnyak, John M. *Birmingham, Toledo's Hungarian Community.* Master's thesis, University of Toledo, 1975.

Jeanquart, Wilford. Interview, Toledo, O. April 19, 1990.

Jubilate—1899-1924: St. Stephen's Parish Jubilee. Toledo:

American-Hungarian Printing Co., 1924.

Kampis, Antal. *The History of Art in Hungary.* Budapest/London: Corvina Press/Collet's, 1966.

Korda, Thomas. Interview. Toledo, Ohio. April 19, 1990.

Ludanyi, Andrew. "Ethnic Community and Identity: The Birmingham Project." Paper presented to Birmingham Cultural Center, April 3, 1986.

Porter, Tana Mosier. *Toledo Profile: A Sesquicentennial History.* Toledo Sesquicentennial Commission, 1987.

Sarabia, Mary L. "The People of the Cup: A History of Calvin United Church of Christ, Hungarian Reformed." Unpublished manuscript.

Szuch, Yolanda Danyi. "A Church's Response to the Preservation of Ethnic Heritage: Religious Traditions at St. Stephen's Church." In *The Preservation of Ethnic Heritage: An Examination of the Birmingham Experience.* Educational Comment, University of Toledo, College of Education and Allied Professions. 1987.

Upton, Dell and Michael Vlach, eds. *Common Places:*

Readings in American Vernacular Architecture. Athens and London: University of Georgia Press, 1986.

Urban Turf and Ethnic Soul: An American Neighborhood's Struggle for Survival. Videotape. Toledo and Ada, Ohio, the Birmingham Community and Ohio Northern University, 1985.

Volgyes, Ivan. *Hungary: A Nation of Contradictions.* Boulder, Colorado: Westview Press, 1982.

Wuest, Sue A. *Current History Report of Birmingham Neighborhood.* Unpublished manuscript for Urban Visual History Planning course. University of Toledo, Department of Geography and Planning. June, 1986.

Recipes and Ethnic Identity —

Bently, Amy. "Culture and Food." In *Digest: A Review for the Interdisciplinary Study of Food*, 1996.

Camp, Charles. *American Foodways: What, When, Why and How We Eat In America.* Little Rock, Arkansas, 1989.

de la Pena Brown, M. H. "Una Tamalada: The Special

Event." In *Western Folklore 40* (1981), No. 1.

Glassie, Henry. *The Spirit of Folk Art.* Sante Fe: Museum of New Mexico Press, 1989.

Goldman, Judy. "A Moveable Feast: The Art of a Knish Maker." In *Western Folklore 40* (1981), No. 1.

Humphrey, Theodore and Humphrey, Lin. *We Gather Together: Food and Festival in American Life.* Ann Arbor, Michigan: University Microfilm Press, 1988.

Ireland, Lynne. "The Compiled Cookbook as Fooways Autobiography," in *Western Folklore 40* (1981), No. 1.

Kalcik, Susan. "Ethnic Foodways in America: Symbol and the Performance of Identity." In *Ethnic and Regional Foodways in the United States: The Performance of Group Identity,* ed. Linda Keller Brown and Kay Mussell. Knoxville: University of Tennessee Press, 1984.

Lave, Jean, and Wenger, Etienne. *Situated Learning: Legitimate Peripheral Participation.* New York: Cambridge University Press, 1991.

Levin, Judith. "Why Folklorists Should Study Housework," in *Feminist Theory and the Study of Folklore,* Susan Tower Hollis, Linda Pershing, and M. Jane Young, eds. Urbana, Illinois: University of Illinois Press, 1993.

Lockwood, Yvonne, and Lockwood, William. "Pasties in Michigan's Upper Peninsula: Foodways, Interethnic Relations, and Regionalism," in *Creative Ethnicity: Symbols and Strategies of Contemporary Ethnic Life.* Stephen Stern, and John Cicala, eds. Logan, Utah: Utah State University Press, 1991.

Long, Lucy. "Culinary Tourism: A Folkloristic Perspective on Eating and Otherness," in *Southern Folklore 55* (1998), No. 3.

Toelken, Barre. *The Dynamics of Folklore.* Revised edition. Logan, Utah: Utah State University Press, 1996.

Turner, Kay, and Seriff, Suzanne. "'Giving an Altar to St. Joseph': A Feminist Perspective on a Patronal Feast," in *Feminist Theory and the Study of Folklore.* Susan Tower Hollis, Linda Pershing, and M. Jane Young, eds. Urbana, Illinois: University of Illinois Press, 1993.

Van Esterik, Penny. "Feeding Their Faith: Recipe Knowledge among Thai Buddhist Women," in *Food & Foodways 1* (1986), No. 2.

The Sutni Saluna —

Karoly, Viski. *Hungarian Peasant Customs.* 2nd Edition. Budapest: (Athenaeum) Vajna and Co., 1937.

Kirshenblatt-Gimblett, Barbara."Studying Immigrant and Ethnic Lore." In *Handbook of American Folklore*, ed. Richard M. Dorson, Chicago: University of Chicago Press, pp. 39-47.

Konnyu, Leslie. *Hungarians in the United States; An Immigration Study.* St. Louis: American Hungarian Review, 1967.

Ludanyi, Andrew."Preservation of Birmingham's Cultural Heritage: Some Random Thoughts about the 'Sutni' and 'Locsolas' Traditions in Birmingham," in The University of Toledo College of Education and Allied Professions 1987 Educational Comment, ed. John F. Ahern. Toledo: University of Toledo, 1987, pp. 33-42.

The Betlehemes játék Christmas Play —

Bernheimer, Richard. *Wild Men in the Middle Ages.* Cambridge, Massachusetts: Harvard University Press, 1952.

Helm, Alex. "The Rumanian Kalusari Play." In *The English Mummers and Their Plays,* Alan Brody, ed. Philadelphia: Temple University Press, 1970.

Pollack, Rhoda Gale."Angelic Imagery in the English Mystery Cycles."Theatre Notebook, 29 (1975), 124-139.

Rearick, Elizabeth C. *Dances of the Hungarians.* New York: Columbia University Press, 1979.

Young, Karl. *The Drama of the Medieval Church.* London: Oxford University Press, 1933.

Viski, Karoly. *Hungarian Peasant Customs.* Trans. by Judith de Marffy-Mantuano. Budapest, 1932.

About the Contributors

John Ahern is Professor Emeritus, The University of Toledo College of Education. He is a member of the Birmingham Cultural Center Hall of Fame and the editor of *Roots in Birmingham.*

Tom Barden is Professor of English and Associate Dean for the Humanities, the College of Arts and Sciences of the University of Toledo. He is author of *Virginia Folk Legends, The Travels of Peter Woodhouse: Memoir of an American Pioneer,* and editor of *Weevils in the Wheat: Interviews with Virginia Ex-Slaves.* He has conducted folklore fieldwork in Virginia, Wisconsin, Ohio, and Wales.

Kay Blalock received her Ph.D. from the University of Toledo and is an Assistant Professor at St. Louis Community College-Meramec in Missouri. She has written entries for *The Encyclopedia of Irish in America* (University of Notre

Dame Press) and in separate encyclopedias published by ABC-CLIO: *Girlhood in America and The Family in America.* Her interests continue to focus on ethnic female identity in southern communities at the turn of the twentieth century.

Lynne Hamer received her Ph.D. in folklore from Indiana University, and is Associate Professor of Educational Psychology, Research, and Social Foundations in the College of Education at the University of Toledo. She edits *Folklore and Education,* the biannual newsletter of the Folklore and Education Section of the American Folklore Society, and serves on the National Task Force on Folk Arts in Education. This article is based on her first fieldwork in Toledo.

William Kertesz was born and raised in the Birmingham neighborhood to which his Hungarian-born parents had moved in 1915. He joined the U.S. Navy during World War II, then worked for the former Nickle Plate Railroad until

1951. He was a Toledo Fire Department fire fighter until 1981. Mr. Kertesz had a strong interest in history and historical photography and was responsible for the extensive collection of images of the neighborhood currently held by the Birmingham Cultural Center. Before his death in 1996, he gave numerous showings of the photo essay, part of which is reprinted here.

Ted J. Ligibel is the director of Eastern Michigan University's Historic Preservation Program. In 1976, he established the Northwest Ohio Historic Preservation Office through the Ohio Historical Society. A frequent lecturer throughout region, he is the author of *Lights Along the River: Landmark Architecture of the Maumee River Valley; Island Heritage: A Guided Tour to Lake Erie's Bass Islands,* and *The Toledo Zoo's First 100 Years: A Century of Adventure.* He is currently vice-president of the National Council for Preservation Education.

Andrew Ludanyi is Professor of History and Political

Science in the Department of History and Political Science, Ohio Northern University, Ada, Ohio, and an authority on Hungarian culture in the New World. He is co-editor of *Transylvania: The Roots of Ethnic Conflict.*

Raymond Pentzell, who received his doctorate in theater history from Yale University, was Professor of Theater at the University of Toledo when he conducted the research on which "The Betlehemes játék Christmas Play" is based. He moved to Hillsdale College in Michigan in 1982 to become chair of the Department of Theater and Speech and remained in that position until his untimely death, at age 55, in 1996. His section here, his last work, is a revision of a scholarly article he published in *Educational Theater Journal* (May 1977). He was a scholar's scholar, a man of the theater, a beloved teacher, and a whirlwind of fun and energy.

Peter Ujvagi had just started second grade in Budapest, Hungary when the Revolution of 1956 broke out. After a harrowing escape on Christmas Eve, the Ujvagi family arrived in the United States in 1957 and made their way to Toledo. Mr. Ujvagi, an urban affairs expert, has worked with national and federal organizations to strengthen and develop ethnic neighborhoods. He is CEO of E and C Industries and served on Toledo's City Council since 1981. A leader in the Lucas County Democratic Party, Mr. Ujvagi was President of Toledo City Council until November, 2002, when he was elected to the Ohio House of Representatives, representing District 47.

INDEX